EFFORTLESS MONEY

HOW TO ALIGN YOUR WEALTH AND YOUR WOO

By Victoria Sexton

Align Publishing

Paso Robles, CA

Effortless Money: How to Align Your Wealth and Your Woo

For more information, address vsexton@victoriasexton.com.

ISBN: 978-1-7373027-0-4

Printed in the United States of America

Cover design by Stephanie Knight

Edited by Allison Hrip of Aurora Corialis Publishing

Disclaimer

This book is presented solely for educational purposes. The author and those who worked on this book are not offering it as legal, accounting, medical, or other professional services advice. While best efforts have been used in preparing this book, the author and those who worked on this book make no representations or warranties of any kind and assume no liabilities of any kind with respect to the accuracy or completeness of the contents and specifically disclaim any implied warranties of merchantability or fitness of use for a particular purpose.

Neither the author nor those who worked on this book shall be held liable or responsible to any person or entity with respect to any loss or incidental or consequential damages caused, or alleged to have been caused, directly or indirectly, by the information or programs contained herein. No warranty may be created or extended by sales representatives or written sales materials. Every person is different and the advice and strategies contained herein may not be suitable for your situation.

DISCLAIMER

TABLE OF CONTENTS

INTRODUCTION

One day during the mid-pandemic lockdown in 2020, I attended a zoom happy-hour with a women's business group. I was enjoying a glass of wine while one of my friends vented her frustrations about life in general. She said that life seemed hard. And it wasn't just one thing, but life in general seemed more difficult.

The conversation flowed from one topic to another—from kids, to work, to money. We all seemed to have the same experience. Between homeschool, working from home, cooking constantly, trying to avoid cabin fever, and worrying about jobs, money, and the national TP supply, life just seemed to get more complicated.

Finally, my friend yelled out, "Arg, why can't things just be easy! I can't take one more complicated thing right now."

What a question! With it came the best answer ever. I mean, why *can't* things be easy?

This was the answer to every problem my clients were experiencing. Every time they felt frustrated with their financial system, confused by financial terms or unworthy of wealth, this was the over-arching theme.

Why can't things be easy?

Guess what? Even if everything else seems complicated, we can make our money easy.

Let's get real for a second. Sometimes dealing with our money can be hard, scary, or just complicated. And, if you're like me, you're tired of being mansplained. If you're like me, you just want real life solutions, without the fluff. *Effortless money* is more than a catchy slogan, it's a movement to simplify our money and optimize our mindset so we can finally start to make some headway on our financial goals.

Our money can be easy if we decide that's how it's going to be, if we just expect it to be that way. *Effortless money* is the solution for my clients who are struggling to figure out their money, afraid to make financial decisions, or just don't feel worthy of the kind of wealth that they want. I incorporated my favorite money tips and techniques into one system that makes money *easy*.

I hope this book inspires you to bring some *effortless* to your life and to start the rewarding work of developing a better relationship with your money.

Sending you love and good money vibes!

Chapter 1. Why You Need Effortless Money

Why do we over complicate things, especially our money?

Have you ever been at the grocery store at the end of the day and you're feeling a bit frantic? You've had *a day*. It's 5 p.m. and you're standing in the grocery line, kids whining that they're hungry, your significant other on the way home, and all you want to do is get the heck home. You finally get your total, swipe your debit card, and . . .

DECLINED.

What? You ask them to swipe it again.

The checker says, "I'm sorry ma'am, it says insufficient funds." You dig through your purse hoping you have enough cash for the essentials when you remember your spare credit card and swipe it, hoping the person behind you didn't notice you nearly died of embarrassment, right there at checkout number five.

Beep.

"This one went through," the cashier announces loudly, to add to your embarrassment.

You sign a squiggle on the register pad with your finger, anxious to get the heck out of there. You think to yourself that you really need to check your bank balance to find out what's going on with your account. Your kids are talking to you the whole time, taking up brain space—you hear that Megatron might not be a bad Transformer after all, and that octopus have 3 hearts—all while trying not to drop your groceries in the parking lot. Somewhere between the checkout line and getting into your car, you completely forget about your money.

It's no surprise the thought of checking your bank account has left you. Life got in the way and you forgot all about looking at your finances.

This situation happens all the time.

One day I was driving home from my job, and I realized I forgot, again, to pay a bill. I received one of *those* notices from the electric company: you know the kind, it that says you have five days to pay your power bill before it gets shut off.

ARG!

I felt so stupid. I felt like I should have done better. I felt like I should have *known* better, because at the time, I was a financial advisor.

I mean, I was helping people with their money every day, yet I forgot to pay one of my own bills. How does that happen? After a few minutes of shaming and judging myself, I realized if I were my own client, shame wouldn't be a part of the conversation. If the roles were reversed, I would tell her she's too stinkin' busy, and to give herself some grace.

I would also tell her to get as organized as she could, to simplify things until they could no longer be simplified, and to make things as easy as possible for herself. That way, mistakes happen less frequently, and when they do, it won't be a huge deal. I would tell my client to stop beating herself up because nothing good comes from shaming, blaming, and judging yourself.

There's a difference between knowing better and doing better. Really, I guess we all should know better. If you have ever read any personal finance articles, you've heard the standard advice: have an emergency savings, save for retirement, and live below your means. We *should* know this stuff, but the reality is our lives are complicated and, after March 2020, our lives got even more complicated.

Between sanitizing everyone after they come home and parents homeschooling their kids while still working, the areas in our lives on the verge of falling apart have become extremely clear. For many of us, a major area of stress is money. Maybe we don't make enough money to cover our bills, or we have no idea where our financial documents are, or maybe we just feel like we're not very good at this whole money thing. Our financial situation, and how we feel about it, is now clearer than ever. The upside to identifying something isn't working is you have no place to go but up.

Right now, it's even more important that we simplify our money so we can make our lives a little bit easier. By making our money effortless, we can stop stressing. Maybe you can stop writing lists each day of all the things you have to do, or maybe you can sleep soundly knowing all your bills are paid for the month.

Simplifying your money is one of the greatest gifts you can give yourself. In simplifying your money, you're getting your financial house in order, and you become more prepared for what life may throw at you. This creates a foundation for doing very adult things like investing and financial planning. Simplifying your money also means you will be less likely to overlook your money or leave money on the table.

For many of us, we think personal finance is super complicated, like we need a professional to make our financial decisions. While an advisor may be helpful, it's important to know that *you* have the ability to manage your own finances. Even if you don't end up managing your money and outsource the task, you have the capability to do so. It is possible for you to achieve *effortless money*.

Why You Need Effortless Money

Let's make something clear, effortless money doesn't mean you can sit on the couch all day and money will fall in your lap. Effortless money means you're not stressed about your money all the time, you're making headway on your financial goals, and you have a plan for the unexpected. You know where you stand, so when life happens, you're not completely devastated.

Your *effortless money* will only take a short time to set up. Once established, you will know your financial plan, and have a road map to wealth. You will learn to leverage your mindset, and you'll be able to tap into your wealthy future self.

There are some basic steps to effortless money. In this book we'll cover:

1) Money Mindset - everything starts with your mindset. What you believe is your reality. If you believe you will never experience wealth, then you will never experience wealth.
2) Money Simplicity System - get yourself organized and set for success. You can't take over the world if you're a wreck. Let's get you organized with a simple system that makes sense to you.
3) Inner Wealthy Woman - tap into your inner wealthy woman. If you can visualize it, you can create it. Athletes and high performers have been using visualization for years to help them achieve their goals, and you can too.

While this gives you a head start, this is just an introduction to effortless money. You can get more information, and grab my checklist to get you on the path to *Effortless Money in Just 5 Minutes a Day*: victoriasexton.com/five.

The Ebb and Flow of Effortless Money

If you've ever talked with anyone about *being in flow*, you know that flow is a concept of ease in accepting abundance, being productive, and receiving good things into your life.

There's also a flow to money.

Many people experience an outward flow of money, but don't as easily experience an inward flow of money. This means that money leaves your hands easily but doesn't come to you at such a rapid pace. If you've been taught that *money doesn't grow on trees* or *you never get something for nothing,* you might find it hard to experience an inward flow of money.

I've found that sometimes a rapid outward flow of money can be unnerving and even throw you off your game. It can seem like the outward flow of money will never stop. For me, that's when panic sets in. It's times like those that I need to stop and reset before I completely go down the rabbit hole.

There's both an ebb and flow to money, just like the ocean. Assuming that the ebb is going to last forever means you're actually expecting things to continue to get worse. Sometimes you can actually manifest not-so-great things to happen because you're so concentrated on it.

It's OK for money to go out. It's part of the ebb and flow of money. I've found that the ebb of money is much easier when you have a plan, and you understand that the flow will happen too. Remember, sometimes there's a huge ebb, right before a big wave comes in.

Why Money Is Never Just Money

After spending 20 years in the corporate world, I became a financial advisor and began helping individuals with their money. One of the things I learned very quickly is that money is never just about money. Money is always about the things that it represents. Money is about our family: how we were raised our beliefs, values, the things we tell ourselves, our relationship with our parents, and so much more. At times, we can get tripped up when we try to change our dynamic with money, such as how much we make, throwing us for a loop.

Let's say you want to make more money. This sounds simple, right? You just make more money, don't you?

I've experienced many people in my life, clients and otherwise, who say things like, *I've never made over $75,000 a year*, or whatever the number is, and sometimes, if they did make over that amount, crazy things would happen. Maybe their car would break down, or a pipe would burst in their house, or they received a big bill. Sometimes these things would happen all that the same time.

It would be as if there were a magical bank somewhere saying, *Hey, you went over your $75,000, so we balanced things out for you.*

While there is no mystical magical bank—unfortunately—I do know that we frequently block ourselves from our abundance, prosperity, and making more money. We can block our abundance without understanding what we're doing. We do it out of fear and habit and trying hard to be logical, which sometimes conflicts with our gut.

Our brains may seem like they're in charge of the show with our money, but honestly, they aren't. Our brains only have one bit of the equation. As you'll find in this book, our money isn't just determined by our salary, but our mindset, our beliefs, and our energy around money, as well.

Here's a question you may be thinking: *So, if money is never just about money, what the heck is it about*?

I am very pragmatic. I understand investments, and the mechanics of making money, but I also understand money is emotional. Money is familial. Money is habitual and money is about a million other things, too. It's not until you realize your money isn't just money, and align yourself with your flow of money, that you will experience true abundance.

You can be as pragmatic with your money as you want to be, but until you delve into the deeper issues holding you back from wealth, you are not going to get to the root of the problem or find yourself on the other side of your financial situation. This doesn't mean you need to go to therapy to find out why you're not making the money you want, but it does mean it might serve you well to acknowledge your money issues may be deeper than you anticipated.

The Start of Effortless Money

I quit my job and decided to start my own business, but honestly, I was a little scared. OK, I was a lot scared. I didn't really know what products or services I was going to offer. What I did know was I had a deep desire to help people, and I could *not* bear to be in another corporate job where I would have to listen to yet another man patronize me about how I need to do things the *company way*. I was tired of that bullshit and knew I needed to work for myself.

So, there I was, trying to figure out what financial courses and tools to offer my clients, when I received a random email. A lady who I met through a networking group knew about my love of crystals. I put together a *crystals for wealth* crystal bag as a fun holiday gift for clients. The same lady randomly emailed me and asked if I could put together a custom crystal bag for her sister.

What?

She knew how much I liked crystals and thought it would be an amazing idea to put together a custom crystal bag for her sister's birthday. I thought it was such a random request. I hadn't yet returned her email and was telling a friend about how I was going to turn it down. I mean, my job isn't crystals. What a random thing to ask me. I was telling a friend all about it when she started to yell at me, in a playful way.

She said, "Stop blocking your abundance! Someone's trying to pay you, let them."

The irony of the scenario is that I say those words to clients all the time, yet no one had ever said them back to me. Just like when my kids quote my own wisdom back to me (so delightful), she was quoting *me* back to *me*.

It was very simple. The lady from my networking group wanted to pay me for something that I enjoy doing already. I should let her. End of story.

I decided to accept the nice lady's offer, put together a crystal gift basket for her sister, and sent it out to the East Coast before I could think too much about it. That week, I decided I needed to focus on NOT blocking my abundance. Heck, if someone wants to pay me for something I do anyway, why shouldn't I let them?

From then on, my money mantra was *easy money*. Every time I felt myself start to lean toward fear or anxiety or *oh shit, I haven't done this before*! I would take a deep breath and repeat my mantra, *Easy. Money.*

I started repeating *easy money* to myself every time I began to freak out over money or my business. I would sometimes switch it up and add details: *easy money comes to me effortlessly, easy money is on the way,* or even, *I'm ready for easy money.*

I realized that I didn't want just easy money. Easy money sounded like a band aid or a quick fix. I realized I wanted money that was so simple it required very little effort. I wanted *effortless money.*

At that time, I didn't realize that *Effortless money* wasn't just a mantra, it became my way of life. *Effortless money* is a way of setting yourself up for success financially. I mean, who doesn't want their money to be effortless? Who doesn't want making money, receiving money, managing money, organizing money, and everything in between to be easy? When we can stop stressing, obsessing, and double-checking our finances, we can free up brain space we've been using in the struggle over our money. This ease frees up time, energy, and resources for us to do the things that we really want to do.

As I worked with more and more clients, I found the concept of *effortless money* came up frequently.

I started to think of how I could make money *effortless* for my clients. I decided to use all the tools, tips, and techniques I learned over the years to make money as simple as possible, helping ease the *freak out* that often happens around money and help clients get back to living their lives. While I can't possibly cram all of my money knowledge into one book, I can get you started on your path to *effortless money.*

THE WOO PART OF EFFORTLESS MONEY

Effortless money means I'm doing my part to make my finances simple. That includes mindset, strategy, and organization. *Effortless money* also means accepting my abundance, living a life of gratitude, and trying to stay in my power.

When you accept abundance into your life, and live with an abundance mentality, you step into the ease and flow of money. You ask for what you want from the universe and are open to receive it. That's not to say you don't have a financial plan; actually, it's important to know what you want. How can you ask for something if you don't know specifically what it is? Asking for something vague will get you more vague; asking for something specific will get you what you asked for.

Effortless money is my way of establishing a healthy money mindset and healthy goals, along with maintaining organization in a way that will motivate you to keep going with your financial goals.

Why do we need *effortless money* in our lives? The answer is simple: who doesn't want something as boring, daunting, and complicated as your finances to be easy and effortless? If we want an easier life, we need to make things simple, streamlined, and efficient, and that includes our money.

EFFORTLESS MONEY SHOULD BE EVERYONE'S GOAL

If you could make things easier on yourself, would you? Having an *effortless money* lifestyle doesn't mean you don't have any worries, or that you spend money like you're Beyoncé; it means you try to make things as simple and effortless as possible. I'm excited to share with you my *Effortless Money* techniques, tips, and tricks for making your life, and dealing with your finances, a little bit easier.

Chapter 2. Even a Financial Advisor Needs to Do Their Work

Just Because I Work In Finance Doesn't Mean I've Achieved Perfection

I can remember that when I was 15 years old, I couldn't *wait* to get a job and start making some money. I always had multiple jobs in my teen years: I would dog-sit, housesit, babysit, and wait tables a couple days a week. I was focused on creating income, though I didn't know that at the time. Even now, the act of creating income lights me up. There's something about the energy of making money that's contagious.

My relationship with my dad wasn't a typical one. My dad was a financial consultant, so growing up with him meant we talked about money, investing, and the stock market. Instead of going to father-daughter dances or going out for fro-yo, we read the Wall Street Journal and picked stocks. He taught me what he knew, and he knew money.

By age 18, I opened a Roth IRA with money I had saved from working at the neighborhood Italian deli over Christmas break. It was about that time that I realized what investing really meant. I opened a brokerage account and put in money (money I would have otherwise left in my savings account). I bought mutual funds or stocks. Over time, as the market went up, my investments went up with it. I realized the steps to investing: I put money in, I pick investments—and provided that they do well—my investment grows *way* more than if I had left it in my savings account. Once I figured out how it worked, I was hooked.

I went on to do all the things that I *should*, according to parental standards, like get a college degree, work in corporate America, and attained master's degree. I found myself in my 20s making solid choices, doing what the financial experts say you should be doing, but I still didn't feel like I had a good handle on my money.

I had this feeling like the bottom was going to drop out, all the time. I was worried about money, my credit card balance, and my bills. I didn't know why my beliefs and actions about my money seemed so incongruent. I knew a lot about money, and I did all the things you *should* do. So why did I feel poor? Why was money always coming in and then going right back out? I had an MBA and a fancy job but still didn't feel like I had it all together. What I had yet to realize was that getting in the flow of making money happens fast and just as quickly the flow can be blocked.

When I was in my early 40s, my husband and I decided to quit our corporate jobs and move to a small town on the California Central Coast. I received a job offer to be a financial advisor in the area. I'm going to blame my love of the movie *Working Girl* during my teen years, but honestly, I had always wanted to be a stockbroker. I love the stock market and I want everyone else to love investing, too. The time that I spent with my father growing up (reading the Wall Street Journal and researching stocks) would be well spent.

It was then I got some interesting experience helping women with their money. During my time as an advisor, I found I was spending much of my day talking with women about why they felt so messed up and afraid around money; why they felt that they couldn't hold onto their money; or why they felt like they were telling their money to kick rocks.

What I found working with amazing successful women, who were also struggling with their finances, is that they can't see their own brilliance. They don't see how smart, capable, and financially competent they are. It can be difficult for some women to get past their emotional blocks so they can embody the wealthy woman of their dreams.

THE (SPIRITUAL) ADVISOR

When I was a financial advisor, many times I would tip toe around what I believed to be the problem. I would think *I'm not a therapist or a counselor, I'm their financial advisor.* The reality is that my spiritual beliefs coincide with my monetary beliefs, and sometimes, the discussions were deep, resulting in more thought than action. Financial advisors get paid to make transactions, not to have conversations, but the answer was always in the conversation.

There's an undeniable spiritual connection between us and our money. For some people, their money is never enough, they always want more. For others, they're satisfied with a small salary. I've always thought that there's a correlation between feeling fulfilled in life and your level of satisfaction with your money.

Have you ever had a friend who took a job because the money was good? The money was so good your friend took a job that she hated, thinking she would stay in the job for a year or so, save money, then leave the job, and figure out something else that she might like. Have you noticed that it never ends up working out exactly has your friend expected?

When you do something you dislike, hate, or even loathe for the money, there will never be enough to make up for the unhappy feelings you experience every day. I get it. The job sounds great on paper, but the money you get from that job will never bring you the happiness you might have by leaning into your joy and finding out what you really should be doing instead.

In short, money not only doesn't buy happiness, but it leaves a gaping hole in your soul where your happiness should be. I've taken the job that seems really great on paper. Not only was I miserable, but I also tried to fill up my empty soul with material things, and we all know by now that never works.

When you are able to use your money as a tool to do good for yourself and your community, it comes with an inherent sense of fulfillment. When you have a job you enjoy—even if the money doesn't afford you lavish trips or the ability to buy that Porsche you've dreamed of—you're feeding your soul, and that's something the fancy job could never provide. That's why you feel unfulfilled.

There's a complex connection between who we are and our money. Our money doesn't define us, but what we do for our money and with our money does.

I started sharing this information with my clients. Once my clients and I were on the same page—that there is a spiritual and even energetic connection with our money—we could make a customized financial plan that aligned with their feelings about money and addressed deeper money concerns. When I spend quality time with my clients, and we have established the trust to talk about what's been holding them back financially, that's when financial planning gets magical. We can determine how to make, save, and spend money in a way that feels authentic. It's at that point, we can take a big breath and start to relax; there's a plan, clarity, and a path forward.

How I Stumbled Upon My Money Mojo

I was driving home from work one day—by work, I mean my job as a financial advisor—and, because I'm one of those people with a running list in my head of what I should be doing on any given day, as I was going over my list, I remembered that I forgot to pay the PG&E bill. Again.

It wasn't just a bill, it was one of those bills that said I hadn't paid in a few months. For 3 months, I failed to make a payment, not because I didn't have the money, but because I couldn't remember to pay the dang bill. I meant to pay it, and I actually thought I had. I only realized when I saw the bill that I hadn't paid it.

I found myself in a shame spiral. I kept thinking *shouldn't I know better?* I mean, I was managing millions of dollars but how is it that I couldn't remember to pay the freaking PG&E bill?

I realized I was shaming myself in a major way over this stinking PG&E bill that wasn't even $100.00. How can I possibly be shaming myself this badly over $100.00? Was the shame helping me in any way? Was it motivating me to pay my bills on time? Or was the shame just making me feel small?

During my car ride home, I took stock of the situation. I mean, I'm not a worthless human being. Like most working moms, I'm freaking busy! And I'm human. Humans sometimes forget things.

I started to think about how I approached my money. Maybe all the *should's* weren't working for me. Maybe shaming myself for all the things I *should* be doing isn't actually a motivator. Maybe the *should's* just make me feel bad about myself.

I suddenly had a million questions about how I approached my money. I wondered if I had been going about this all wrong. I remembered a conversation I was having with my 10-year-old son. He was so proud to tell me that he had learned that energy can neither be created nor destroyed. Money, like everything else, is just energy. Energy isn't good or bad, it just *is*.

Money is just a made-up thing that our society established to exchange goods and services. Money isn't really the bad guy. Money isn't out to get you. Money isn't waiting until your car breaks down to hop out of the bushes and say, *guess what? You need a new dishwasher, too.*

If money is just energy, and it's neither good nor bad, then why do we make our money out to be villain? It's almost as if some people think that money likes to hang out with rich people, but not regular folks. Are we actually vilifying our money? Why are we so scared of our money? And why are we NOT leveraging our money to be a creative machine for us?

Since money is just energy, it was then that I realized a similarity between money and humans. Money is energy. People are energy. I thought, if money is energy and people are energy, how can I cultivate a relationship with my money that makes me feel less burdened, more empowered, and even free?

I started to think about how I could cultivate a better relationship with my money. I let my mind reflect on that for a minute. If my money were a person, it would be different, right? We could just have a conversation and then my money would understand I want more easy money in my life and less stress, like wondering if I really did pay the PG&E bill.

Fortunately for me, my imagination is very good at running wild, so I was easily able to imagine what my money would look like if it were actually a person. My money looks like a stack of hundred-dollar bills in cartoon form, with cartoon eyes, Mickey Mouse hands, and don't forget some gold chains.

After I got home from my drive, I decided to and try to have a conversation with my money. I took a deep breath and meditated on my money. Our conversation went something like this.

"Hey Money, so I really like having you around. Do you think that you can ... multiply or something? Or maybe just stick around more often?"

What was interesting is that my money responded.

My money said, "Hey Baby (sounding just like Barry White). Don't you worry. There's more of me where that came from."

Barry and I continued our discussion of mutual admiration and, well, love. I told him how much I loved it when he stuck around and helped me unexpectedly with my bills and expenses. And he reinforced that he would take care of me.

As a result of this conversation, I realized I could have whatever kind of relationship I wanted to have with my money. It could be scary and tense or I could talk with Barry, who would call me *baby* and tell me everything is going to be OK.

I'll take door number two please!

Here's What I learned from My Conversation with Barry

Surprisingly enough, my conversation with Barry (aka—my money) was a loving conversation. I expressed concern and Barry told me he had it covered. What was interesting was there was no fear, no anger, no resentfulness, and no shame. I realized that the fear and shame I experience was entirely self-inflicted and maybe it was about time to let those old habits go.

All those times I cringed as I checked my bank balance, or sighed at my spending, or expressed any negative emotion toward my money, I was perpetuating negative emotions and negative vibes toward my money.

When it came to connecting with my money, I let my fear take control. Instead of leading with the knowledge that everything will be OK, I lead with fear—fear I would never have enough money, fear I was messing up (despite my knowledge), and fear I couldn't instill change in my life. I realized that I was going about it all wrong. Fear was keeping me scared and shameful. Fear was my impediment to living freely and abundantly with my money.

Something else struck me about my conversation with Barry. Even though I have a background in finance, I'm really quick to judge *myself* in relation to my money. I realized, judging myself was getting in the way of enjoying my journey to wealth.

For some reason, people think if you work in finance, you have your money entirely figured out, but that's not always true. I've had to overcome my own share of money struggles. What I learned from my experience was that I needed to shift my mindset. I decided to develop a relationship with my money. When I made this mental shift, something changed for me.

Since my experience with Barry, I learned feelings of anxiety, fear, and shame aren't doing me any good. They aren't serving me at all. If my feelings, and consequently my actions, aren't serving me, I should stop it. I wanted to learn *how* to tap into my money and feel calm, like everything's going to be OK... just like Barry told me it would.

How You Feel About Your Money Matters

How you feel about your money is a giant signal to the universe. By concentrating on something (good or bad), it's a sign to the universe that says, *more please*. You essentially tell the universe that you love something or hate something based upon how much time and effort you give to it. Sound complicated? It's really not. I'll give you an example.

I had no idea how much I was messing myself up by concentrating on all the things I *didn't* want in my life. For years, when I checked my bank balance, I would have some sort of emotion. I would get mad at myself for spending too much money. I would get upset for not saving more. I would feel like there was not enough money to go around. I would concentrate on all the negative aspects of my financial situation. Little did I know I was telling the universe I wanted more of what I was getting, and what I was getting was frustration, worry, and the sense I didn't have enough money to go around. I didn't understand I was sending negative energetic signals to the universe.

When you look at your bank balance how do you feel about your money? This many sounds like silly question, but it's really important. Do you look feel gratitude towards your money or are you always frustrated that there's never enough to go around. What are you focused on? Is it positive or negative?

Focus on how you *want* to feel about your money.

When you focus how you *want* to feel once you achieve your financial goals, you're looking forward to your future and telling the universe to bring you more of what you want.

If you want to feel differently about your money, you have to start acting like that's your current reality. I know this sounds counter-intuitive, but it really does work.

FINDING MY WOO

When I started as a financial advisor, I agreed to take on an office that was already established. The advisor had left the company, but the office was already set up, so they wanted to place another advisor there to ensure client retention. The office came with an assistant. By the time I moved into the office she already had it decorated. You might say that the decor was a cross between grandma's house and a doctor's office from 1990. The office didn't fit my personality at all, but I didn't think too much of it and I got straight to work.

My assistant was in her 70s and reminded me of Roz from the movie *Monsters Inc.* You know, the snail lady who said, "I'm always watching." I don't think that my assistant really got me or my mission. Needless to say she brought the vibe in the office down.

After a year, she thankfully moved on to a different job. The day after she moved, I brought my crystals into the office. I put some black tourmaline, rose quarts, and selenite on her desk to clear out the vibe. Then, I redecorated the office.

From then on, my office reflected my personality and how I work with my clients. I brought in succulents, more crystals, and modern furniture. I put books on my coffee table that I found to be super helpful. They were not only about money, but energy, and women's empowerment.

I noticed that most of my clients found it refreshing to see the changes in my office. It also seemed to give them permission to let their spiritual-freak flag fly, too. It was like my new decor gave my clients permission to let their guard down and they could see who I really am. My clients and I began to have much deeper conversations about not only money, but life, too.

Conversations included aligning their money-making abilities with their life purpose and how they could sustain such money-making practices over time. Some female clients even asked me how could they afford to leave their husbands, or if they should try to stay and stick it out.

As a financial advisor, those were not questions I was paid to answer. I was supposed to be the investment person. I got paid by selling investments. Period. I was not supposed to be their life coach, talking about life purposes, and helping them figure out if they should stay with their husbands. This was my first clue that my job was not right for me.

One thing I noticed as I leaned into being 100% authentic with my clients is that the sweet spot of financial abundance lies in the combination of the practical and the woo—the pragmatic and the spiritual. When you align your actions, your beliefs, and your values and trust in the universe, that's when amazing prosperity happens.

I leaned into my spiritual side. This is the side of me that trusts what my gut is telling me. I found that when my clients and I were each open to listening to our gut, financial planning not only seemed lighter and easier, but things seemed to work out better than we anticipated. When I had to prove to my clients the benefits of savings or investing, our professional relationship, and their desire to become financially secure, fell apart in spectacular ways.

I also started to attract clients who were more in tune with their gut and loved the woo part of financial planning. The more I leaned into woo, the more I found my people. These were clients I loved working with, who also loved working with me, but doing business this way didn't represent the stiff, corporate side of my financial advisement company. I realized to show up fully, authentically, and most effectively for my clients, I really needed to do my own thing.

My Jump into the Deep End

Around the time my woo and my clients were buzzing right along, the pandemic hit full force. People started calling me, completely out of the blue, with questions like, *Should I sell my vacation rental?* to *Should I start that business I've always wanted to*? Not only was there this huge health crisis, but amongst my clients, there was a crisis of the soul. No longer did the mediocre job matter. Suddenly, the boyfriend who never calls no longer made the cut. My clients wanted more: a deeper, more fulfilling life, and part of that included aligning their money with the rest of their dreams and desires.

You don't normally hear people who are straightforward, pragmatic, and all business, talk about the connection between money, energy, and woo. There seems to be little crossover between woo and money. The more I connected the two things for myself, the more I shared it with my financial clients, and the more I was convinced that there was a connection. Their reactions were everything from excitement and relief to amazement and thinking I'm totally nuts.

I never have been one for conformity. I always listen to my gut and my gut was telling me to get the hell out of my corporate job. My gut was telling me that women needed support and I could offer it to them. My gut was telling me, more than ever, women need to connect their woo, their abundance, and their money, and I decided I was going to be the one to help them. So, during the scary pandemic, I told my company to go kick rocks and started my own consulting firm.

Why It Is Important to Connect Wealth to Woo

I know what you're thinking . . . I'm sure that sounds all good and nice, but really, how do you combine your woo with the practical side of money? How do you combine pragmatism and woo? How do you connect your money and your mojo?

I was having a consultation in my office one day. The woman I was chatting with went into detail about how she wanted to make more money. She was making a certain amount of money from her business, let's say $80,000, and she really wanted to make $100,000 a year from her business. The interesting thing was she had no shortage of potential contacts. As a matter of fact, companies were calling her asking her to do work for them. She told me how she was offered a contract but didn't think it *really* fell under her specialty. I mean, she hadn't done that exact thing in the past. She had only done something super-duper similar. She used this as an excuse to not bid on the contact. She said, "I shouldn't bid for the contract, right?"

I was sympathetically listening to her when, finally, something in me was done with the conversation. Before I could even stop the words from coming out of my mouth I said, "Stop telling your money to fuck off." I was almost just as shocked at the words that came out of my mouth as she was, but it was probably the most honest thing that I said to her in the entire hour I was with her.

I tried to recover, but it didn't matter. I could tell she didn't appreciate the fact that I just dropped an eff bomb on her and told her that she was blocking her own success. Not only did she not understand what I was talking about, but her initial reaction was to tell me that I was *just wrong* and didn't understand the situation. It's no shock that I never saw her again.

What I learned quickly from my clients is you can block your abundance a lot faster than you might think. Frequently, we decide that we want something, like more money or more clients, then we end up blocking that new business with our own insecurities, fears, and worries.

Your money is not independent of the rest of your life, including your spiritual life. Somehow, we think that money is just about the numbers, but money is related to so many other things, such as your values and beliefs, your self-worth, your work ethic, and more.

From a logical perspective, it seems like a really weird thing to combine your woo and your wealth, but it makes perfect sense. If we can get a leg up on how we make, save, and spend our money, then why the heck shouldn't we connect our money to our woo? Connecting with your woo is a shortcut to having a better relationship with your money. A better relationship with your money is the key to having more of it, and less stress. Think of it like money therapy.

Money seems so straightforward. You save every month, you clip coupons, you follow the advice of the experts who tell you what you *should* do, and then your financial life is gravy, right? Sometimes, you can follow the advice of every money expert, check all the boxes, and still struggle with your money. This is because money is never just about the cash. Money is like an iceberg, there's always something below the surface.

Some things below the surface might include our beliefs, values, things we tell ourselves about our money, and experiences we had from childhood and the rest of our lives. It's important to understand what money represents your values, too. When you do something with your money in a way that isn't aligned with your values, things never seem to work out. I had one client who came to see me. She purchased an investment from someone, and it hadn't returned very much in the past five years. She said, "I knew it. I knew that was the wrong investment for me."

She knew more than she thought she did. She knew that the investment wasn't aligned with her values and that was enough to know that it wasn't the right investment for her. Aligning your money with your beliefs, values, and everything below the surface of the iceberg is a shortcut to success. Many people feel they don't have the knowledge to do that on their own, but they're wrong.

Chapter 3. What the Heck Is Woo and What Does It Have to Do with My Money?

What Exactly Is "Woo"?

If you've heard of words like "woo," "mojo," "juju," or "special sauce" (my personal favorite), then you know it's really hard to describe the term. I've heard of definitions like *magic* or *charms* or *something indescribable or unexplainable*. When I talk about woo, specifically related your money, I'm talking about more than just believing in the unbelievable, but also, concepts like having faith in the universe, because everything will be OK.

Part of your woo is believing in abundance and that there's enough business, money, and resources for everyone. Another part of your woo is gratitude and appreciation for the things you have in your life and what you will receive in the future—and that's just the start. Woo is believing in yourself and your abilities. Woo is living a courageous and audacious life where you refuse to let fear rule you.

I would like to give you one definition of the *woo of wealth*, but there isn't one specifically. I would say it's the belief that you're capable of having rich experiences, relationships, and an overall rich lifestyle. As a matter of fact, you're not only capable of this but it's within your reach.

This one life you're living is counting on you. You can't possibly live your life to the fullest if you're busy thinking you're not worthy to receive money or that a life rich in money, love, friendships, and experiences is just not possible for you. When you get over your money junk, you can experience richness in your life that is not just momentary, but the kind of richness that stays with you for the rest of your life. Getting over a money-junk mindset is a gift you can give yourself.

What Does Your Vibe Have to Do with Your Money?

Have you ever noticed your vibe is super important? Your vibe can tell someone a million things about you, even before you say a word. Your vibe is not only your attitude; it's your frequency.

If you aren't familiar with the word *vibration*, think of it this way: Let's say you're sitting on the couch surfing Netflix and feeling kind of *meh*. You don't have motivation to do much of anything, but you decide to play your favorite song. You tap your toe, maybe dance, maybe sing, and suddenly, you have renewed energy.

This isn't motivation. This is an example of how your vibe plays a big part in your life. If you're not concentrating on trying to keep your vibe high, you may not even realize you're in a ho-hum, low-vibe state.

When you're in a low-vibe state, you can't see the amazing things around you. Gratitude seems useless. Cultivating relationships with people is more difficult. In my experience, when my vibe is low, bringing in new business is a lot more difficult.

As you might have guessed, a high vibe can change the outcome of your day. Likewise, your money vibe is as important as your money habits. Just like the example above, when you're feeling really *meh* about your money, you will receive *meh* in return.

When you're able to tap into your wealth woo, you feel good about your money. It's that good feeling, that high vibe, that attracts more opportunity and more similar experiences to you. That high-vibe state, where you're feelin' yourself, is the place to be. That's when amazing, synchronicities happen. When you can tap into your mojo, your financial life gets easier.

How to Raise Your Vibe around Money?

For about a year, I conducted my own little experiment. I wondered how changing my vibe would impact my business and the number of new clients I would bring in over the course of the week. I wanted to determine if my vibe positively impacted my relationships with people, and therefore my business?

I started to just focus on my vibe, instead of sales quotas or numbers or graphs or charts. I tried my best to ignore the outcomes, results, and money I would make from each potential client. My intention was to be of service to people through my business. My intention was to increase my vibe to make it easier for people who needed me to find me. It became my full time job to keep my vibe high and see what the universe would bring.

Here are a couple of things I noticed when I tried to keep my vibe high:

1) It's *way* easier to manifest when your vibe is high.

If you've ever tried to manifest anything, you know that there's a fine line between holding on to the outcome and, well, manifesting what you want. That fine line has to do with how much we force the dang thing to happen, whether or not it's the best thing for us. It's easier to manifest when we're not tied to specific outcome. Rather, just concentrate on keeping your vibe high and keeping an open mind.

2) People want to be around high-vibe people.

People want to be around other people who have a high vibe. The practical part of me would sometimes get frustrated at work, because my sometimes really great meetings didn't result in business. I was so confused. I finally realized people want to be around people who make them feel good, and how could I get upset at that? After that, I tried my best to keep my vibe high, try my best to be of service and not worry about the outcome. Whenever that's my focus, the outcome always ends up better than I ever anticipated.

3) When you are in a high-vibe state, anything is possible.

When you're in a high-vibe state, you can't help but be positive. There's something about having a super-awesome high-vibe day that makes you believe anything is possible. It's that belief that brings about magical results.

4) A high vibe fosters creativity.

Possibility seems to be pouring out of your fingertips when you're in a high-vibe state. It was almost like I could see clearly that there was more than one way to accomplish my goal. The possibility, creativity, and opportunities were boundless.

5) Showing up with a high vibe increases business. I was more likely to make a business connection with someone who was like minded. I was able to tell people energetically who I was and what I was about, without saying a word. Likewise, I was able to tell quickly if they were an ideal client for me.

All of that is good and well but how do you change your vibe around your money?

The easiest way I've found to change my vibe around my money is to physically change things up. If you're feeling stagnant, stand up and go for a walk. Listen to your favorite music. Do the thing that you love to do - bake, make art, get as creative as you possible can.

Sometimes the art of creation helps change your energy, which is why it's helpful to find your thing. What do you absolutely love to do? Maybe it's as simple as going for a walk or listening to your favorite music. Change the energy around you and see how it impacts you and your vibe. Get up and move your body. Dance! Get excited about the future!

If you have no idea how to increase your vibe, much less what your vibe is, make it your goal just to keep your energy high and do more of the things that bring you joy. Keep leaning toward the tasks that make you feel good. What gives you that tingly warm, fuzzy feeling?

When you're doing the work that you were meant to do, it feels good. There's a certain ease to it you may not feel doing other tasks. That level of ease, that type of good vibe, is your woo. And guess what? Everyone has woo. What brings you pure joy in life? What makes you feel young and puts a smile on your face? Do more of that.

We Make Our Own Reality

My dad has this saying– *we make our own hell*–and it's especially true of money. The things we believe and tell ourselves, end up becoming our reality.

I was at a lunchtime networking event one day. I frankly wasn't concerned about where I should sit because I was starving. I hit the buffet line and then quickly found an open seat after securing my meal. Most ladies put down a purse indicating their seat was spoken for. When I sat down at the table with my lunch, I had no idea who I was sitting next to. I was at the table alone, snarfing down my lunch, when a nice older lady sat down next to me. We made small talk for a bit. After a while, she turned to me and said, "no one ever taught me how to save money."

YIKES! That one line defined her life. *No one taught me how to save money*, was her way of saying that she never learned good habits from her family, didn't make it a priority to learn them, and never saved herself from bad inherited habits.

No matter how amazing your family is, there's probably some way in which you still need to learn about money. There's probably something you needed to learn on your own. Maybe it's about the mechanics of money, or taking care of yourself, or investing, or whatever it may be. You can either focus on what your childhood didn't provide, or you can learn those lessons now and set yourself up for success going forward.

You can make your own reality. Why not make one that's prosperous and joyful, not fearful and uncertain?

When You Fear Your Money, You Are Telling the Universe You Don't Want It.

It took me a while to realize we're always sending out subtle messages to the universe about our money. We do this by the amount of time we focus our attention on something. If you're someone who frets—and I feel you, I'm a reformed fretter myself—one of the biggest challenges comes in the form of your attention.

I didn't realize that I was giving the universe signals. The signal was that I was so focused on worry that I clearly wanted more worry.

Recently, someone admitted to me that she always ignores her money. She does this intentionally hoping things will just *work out,* and they often do

"Whenever I look at my money, I get so stressed out and that's always when I end up bouncing a check or something. But if I don't ever look at my money, and just assume that money is in my account, it is."

The reason things *work out* with her money when she doesn't look at it, is because she assumes that they will. That focus and attention on everything *working out*, is a signal to the universe saying, *Hey, I know you've got me, so I'm going to assume that it's taken care of.*

There's no magic in ignoring her money. It's not the knowing about her money that causes problems, it's when the doubt comes in and overshadows everything else. When her conviction waivers, and she starts focusing on her bills, she blocks her abundance so badly that the money problems sneak up on her.

I'll admit to you that when I first figured this out, I was super annoyed. What? Why would I want more worry? Or bills? Or car break downs? Or money problems? That makes no sense.

It may not make sense on a logical level, but it actually makes perfect sense on an energetic level. Remember, all things are energy.

When You Have Joy and Gratitude around Your Money, You're Telling the Universe to Bring a Round of Seconds.

Gratitude is a signal to the universe that you really love what you have. When you find ways to be grateful for your money, you're telling the universe you want more of that money, trip, prosperity, whatever it is you love.

Leaning into your gratitude is the easiest way to signal to the universe that you are focused on what you want, love what you have, and would like more. I try to incorporate my gratitude practice into my daily journaling routine.

Instead of being grateful for the big things, I try to be grateful for the small, minute details that sometimes get lost in the shuffle, like fresh cut grass or a beautiful blue sky. See how many things you can appreciate today! Then notice how it makes a change in your day. You would be surprised how this simple shift will make a positive impact on your day.

You Have to Make Peace with Your Money, If You Ever Want Your Financial Situation to Change.

For most people, money is a scary thing. Money is the cause of agony, stress, and worry. People worry about money not lasting. People are afraid to spend their money once they get it. Sometimes we feel bad if we have more money than others or guilty if we spend the money we have. Every day we have a million thoughts, emotions, and beliefs about our money. It wasn't until I realized I could change my perspective, and consequently my relationship with money, that things started to shift for me.

Here's a little secret: for years, I struggled with my money. It's not that I didn't make good money, as a matter of fact, for much of my adult life I've made really good money. I knew what I *should* be doing with my money, but I never felt like I had a handle on my money. It never felt like there was enough. There were always too many bills and never enough cash. I had to make peace with my money before I could experience prosperity.

In 2012 my husband and I took job transfers to Seattle. We were living in the Midwest at the time, but after a tornado came through our backyard, I was open to relocation. The company we both worked for seemed to have more opportunities in Seattle and offered a relocation package. It took us almost a year to find a house that we liked in a reasonably priced neighborhood. Real estate had absolutely boomed in Seattle, making it hard to find a moderately priced house, even in the suburbs.

The thing about financial decisions, and it's true of any decision for that matter, is you only know what you know. We bought a house that needed a little TLC but seemed to have good bones. All we can do is make an informed decision based upon the information that we have. That's it.

Little did we know that over the next five years we would spend $70,000 in unexpected home repairs. Between shoddy DIY projects completed by the previous owner (by the way, never DIY a roof) and neglect, we were drowning in home repairs. With each year we lived in the house, the home repair bill continued to grow.

By June 2016, I had reached my limit with the money-pit house. There was a small spot on the ceiling that indicated there was a problem. When the roofer got to work on the roof, he found that the previous owners just put shingles on top of plywood. In Seattle, where it rains most of the year, that's a really bad idea. The roof estimate doubled.

A week before the roofers started work, the main sewer line to the house went out. One Friday evening, while I was having a heart-to-heart with the plumber, asking him when I could flush the toilet next, he explained that since the main sewer line was broken from the house all the way out to the sewer, it would cost us $10,000 to fix. As I wrote out the check, I realized the cash for our Disney cruise literally went down the toilet.

Money was slipping through our fingers at a rapid pace, and it made me wonder how two people with good jobs could feel so helpless with their money. I started to wonder what kind of weekend jobs we could find. It was then that I decided I needed to make peace with my money. I decided to be one of those people who could manifest amazing stuff in their lives. The only way for me to do that was to turn my money info my new BFF.

The first step to money becoming my new bestie, was getting rid of the biggest expense, and that was our house. Over the next year, we gave the house some much needed love and poured more time and money into it. No matter what, we were going to sell that house the next year.

I also read books on money like it was my job. I started focusing on my mindset to see what worked for me and what didn't. It was like a big experiment. If a technique didn't work out, no big deal. I learned something and moved on to another technique.

I would spend my weekends installing hardwood flooring and reading books on how to manifest abundance, wealth, and better money-management skills. I didn't know that time would be the education I needed to shift my mindset and eventually my relationship with money.

The biggest challenge for me was getting some traction. I was dying to see a shift in my relationship with money. If you're in the place where you need to see a shift in your money so you can get going toward your goals, here are few ideas to get the ball rolling.

1) Focus on what you want, not on what you don't. Instead of focusing on the money you don't have, focus on what you do have and what you want more of in your life.

This requires you to think about what you really want. Sometimes when you're in a dark place, having hope is hard, but hope is important. When times have been hard I've said, "6 months from now I'll be in a better place than today." I do this because I have to believe good things are possible for me.

2) Lean into gratitude. Check your bank account and be thankful for every transaction, every bill that was paid, and every coffee that was consumed. The more you can be thankful, the more you're signaling to the universe that you want more of what you're thankful for. So, be thankful.

3) Come up with a money mantra that can help turn your day around. Try something simple like *money comes easily to me* or you can steal my favorite, *easy money flows quickly to me*. You can use this mantra when you find yourself leading with fear, instead of gratitude. To get ideas for a money mantra, go to www.victoriasexton.com/moneyaffirmations.

Chapter 4. The Junk We Tell Ourselves

Before you venture into your relationship with your money and start connecting with your own version of Barry, I think it's important to have an understanding of the things you tell yourself about your money on a daily basis. Each day we talk to ourselves. The things we say to ourselves can really be appalling. I've found that women, especially, have some horrendous self-talk. We say things to ourselves that we would never say to another human being.

We call ourselves stupid, or ugly, or not as good as another person. All the negative self-talk is not helping us achieve our goals in life; it's actually holding us back in a big way. How we talk to ourselves reinforces our fears. The negative self-trash talk really impacts our goals and dreams . . . and not in a good way.

One of the most important things you can do is figure out your primary money story. Money stories sometimes stem from real situations that occur in our lives that are extremely memorable. Many times, we have an underlying money story that reinforces our messed-up relationship with money.

Your money story can be something like a phrase that you heard growing up and now defines your relationship with your money. For example, maybe you heard messages like this growing up, *I can't afford that.* That was my mother's go-to phrase. I don't remember a *maybe we can afford that* or *let's find a way to afford that*. It was always just *we can't afford that*. That was the money story that I had in my head for a long time.

The interesting thing about money stories is that frequently they reinforce a sense of lack or a scarcity mentality.

Many times, your primary money story is the most impactful money memory from your life. It could be that time that you earned enough money to buy that bike you really wanted or the birthday that you didn't get a cake because your parents couldn't afford it.

What Is Your Primary Money Story?

Just like the lady who told me, *no-one ever taught me how to save*, we're reinforcing our money stories all the time. The big question is this: Do you feel like your primary money story represents you? Does it feel like a story that's holding you back or a story that's inspirational and liberating?

Spend some quiet time and identify your primary money story. What have you been telling yourself about your money? Is it something that has been repeated from a parent or grandparent?

Here's the next most important question: Do you want to keep this money story? Does it fit with your life now? Do you want to change it?

Remember, the beautiful thing about stories is that they can be re-written. If your money story is no longer helping you in your life, change it. Just remember that you're the hero of your life and your own story.

One-Liners

If you're anything like me, you have this constant inner monologue going on in your head. For me, the monologue includes things that I need to get done for the day. It also includes my inner reactions to events that happen throughout the day. We're always talking to ourselves about our money. The unfortunate reality is that this inner monologue usually isn't very nice. Most of us would never say out loud the words that we say to ourselves. We let this critical inner voice have a big effect on our lives, because we're actually reinforcing thoughts and beliefs about our money and also our ability to manage our money.

What I call a one-liner is something that you say frequently that just rolls off the tongue like, *money doesn't grow on trees*. One-liners are quick and fast. Something like my mother's, *we can't afford that* is a one-liner. While they may seem harmless, they're actually reinforcing our money beliefs. Often, we say one-liners several times throughout the day, which means that we continue to reinforce our lack and scarcity state, not abundance.

If we're telling ourselves negative junk all day, how do we turn that around into something positive?

One of the easiest ways to turn something negative into something positive is by turning it into a question. Instead of saying something like, *that's too pricey,* you can turn that around into something more positive like, *I would love to be able to afford that.* Or *how can we afford that?* Or *how can I buy that?* Play around with the idea of turning a negative phrase into a positive.

If you're ready to start changing that negative self-talk, write down all of the things you tell yourself about your money over the course of the day. What was your total number of comments? Were all the comments negative? How many were positive? It will surprise you how many of your money thoughts throughout the day are negative.

Is Money Mindset Just Positive Thinking?

You may have heard people talk about money mindset. Most people think that money mindset is just thinking positive. I hate to break it to you, but just thinking positive doesn't really do anything for you. In my experience, just thinking positive frustrates me. I can think positive, and my bills never get paid sooner and my problems never go away.

While thinking positive does sound like a nice new-age way to get in touch with your money, it's sort of like putting a Band-Aid on the problem. The problem is not that you're not thinking positive. Many times, *thinking positive* involves ignoring, deflecting, or pushing down your emotions. You ignore your feelings of anger, frustration, or fear and try to replace it with forced fake happiness. Remember, if the only thing you need to do to achieve your financial goals is think positive, there would be a crap ton of millionaires out there.

I believe that there are two parts to money. The first is the woo, the spiritual part that's driven by what you believe, your values, and life experiences. The second part is the practical, technical, and completely logical side of finances.

Imagine the Grand Canyon. One side of the Grand Canyon is the practical, pragmatic side of money. The other side of the Grand Canyon is the woo, abundance, manifesting side of money. There needs to be a bridge between the two for your money to be easy-peasy.

For years, I was doing the practical, pragmatic things for my money and at the same time I was trying to manifest and get into the woo side of money, but it didn't seem to work. Something always seemed to be lacking, and it became extremely frustrating, especially since I've always worked in finance. I mean, you would think that I have my shit together, right?

It took me a really long time to figure out the formula to bridge the two sides of the Grand Canyon together: meaning a bridge from the practical side of your money and the woo side of your money. I'm going to go over both sides of money in this book.

If you're one of those people who likes all the information and resources, I am here for you. Go to www.victoriasexton.com/resources and grab my free resources. My hope is that this book (along with additional resources on my website) will help bridge the gap between the two sides of your financial Grand Canyon.

Chapter 5. Fear and Money Are Frenemies

Your Fear and Your Money Aren't Friends

The biggest thing that will mess up your money groove is fear. Fear holds you back. Fear stops you from achieving your dreams. Fear makes you feel small, like you'll never accomplish your goals. Fear makes you want to crawl under the covers with a pint of Ben & Jerry's because you will never be able to do *it* anyway.

There's a connection between your fear and your money. Fear holds you back from becoming the best version of yourself. Fear also holds you back from being amazing with your money and makes you second-guess yourself and your decisions.

Fear keeps you from having a better relationship with your money, hence keeping you from being more efficient and making more of it. On an energetic level, money fear is a signal to the universe that you don't want whatever it is that you're afraid of. Energetically, fear is actually pushing your money away.

Fear also keeps us from experiencing new things in our lives. We're so afraid that we don't branch out. In short, fear doesn't help us in any way with our money, and is actually hindering our wealth and abundance.

Everyone has had to deal with fear in some way. I've had to get over my own personal, professional, and financial fears. As harrowing as facing your fears can be, you will never experience financial freedom if you let your fear rule your life. Luckily, the antidote to fear is simple, yet not always easy.

Instead of trying to fight against the fear, recognize your fear. Telling yourself that you aren't scared is a lie, because deep down you know that you're scared. Instead, try to shift your energy. Can you get excited instead of anxious? Or turn your fear into anticipation?

I like to think about fear as an indicator of something new in my life. I take the anxiety of fear as a clue that I'm doing something new and maybe a little bit scary. New things can also be amazing, which is why letting your fear rule you just ends up keeping you small.

The next time you feel afraid, recognize the little tingling in your tummy as a sign that something new is about to happen, and new things—big, huge, scary things—can be exciting. It's that energy of excitement that helps you keep your momentum going while combatting fear. When I tell myself I'm afraid, all of my good creative mojo starts to feel stagnant or off. When I tell myself I'm excited, my energy gains momentum, and that's what you want.

HOW DO YOU GET OVER YOUR FEAR, REALLY?

One thing I've learned about fear is that you're going to feel all the feelings anyway, so you might as well take action. I remember a friend telling me how brave I was. In 2005 my mom suddenly passed away and it was like the bottom dropped out of my entire life. My mom wasn't planning on dying any time soon. She just bought an adorable yellow lab, and suddenly, I had a 5-month-old puppy.

The dog gave me a great lesson. As much as I wanted to crawl under the covers and never climb back out, that wasn't possible. The dog didn't know, nor did she care, that I was going through a life tragedy. At 6 a.m. every morning, she would silently stare at me until I would suddenly wake up. She wanted to go for a walk. The dog got me out of bed every morning and got me physically moving. If you've ever experienced a lab puppy, you know they have the energy of a toddler who just ate a jumbo-size Snickers.

Our daily walks got me physically moving. It was the movement that got me out of my grief. The same can be said for your fear. Action is the antidote to fear. Action makes you realize that the thing you've been so terrified of isn't so scary after all. Taking action can be excruciating. This is why it's a simple solution, but not an easy one.

Action causes you to move past your fear. Action will propel you through the fear to a different place altogether. The act of getting up the nerve to do the thing that *scares the crap out of you*, is the solution to your problem of being scared.

How does this relate to your money? If you're afraid of your money, specifically if you're afraid of dealing with your money, the easiest way to get over that fear is to connect with your money. Check your bank account, make sure you know where your statements are, and start to get organized.

What if that fear is keeping you stuck in the same cycle? At some point in time, you have to tell fear to go pound sand. Your desire to have a different relationship with money has to be bigger than the fear. Sometimes you just have to step into the scary unknown of being in charge of your money. Adulting isn't always fun but having enough money to do things like go on a trip or buy a new house is.

Where's Your Fearless Girl?

There's a bronze statue adjacent to the New York Stock Exchange called *Fearless Girl.* The statue is a girl, probably around 12 years old, wearing a ponytail, skirt, and sneakers with her hands on her hips looking like she is determined to take on the world. That statue reminds me of what women can achieve when we tell our fear to kick rocks.

When I was seven years old, I used to climb trees while wearing a fancy party dress. When I think back to that age, I don't think I was afraid of anything. Like many other women, along the way my insecurities surfaced, and I lost track of my fearless girl. Now that I'm in my 40s, I've tried to tap into that fearless girl again.

I feel like there's a fearless girl inside each one of us. The question is how can we be more fearless with our lives? How can we be more self-assured so that we have the gumption to make big changes? How can we have enough money confidence to believe we're making the right choices? How can you tap into your fearless girl?

You begin by giving yourself the time and space to get back to the person that you were when you felt like you could take on the world. For some of you that is age seven, for others that's in college when you felt like you could do anything. Give yourself time each day to be fearless, even if you start with baby steps.

Baby steps might include listening to the song that makes you feel like a badass or spending less time with people who think that you aren't spectacular and more time with people who do. The trick is to do things that make us feel more like our *true* selves. We all have that friend who thinks that we're amazing, just as we are. Hang out with her or at last pretend like you are.

If you like to journal or meditate, here's an exercise that you can use to tap into your fearless girl. Remember a time where you felt like you could take on the world. You didn't have a sense of *not* being able to do something or a sense of your limitations. You just did it. How did you feel at that time? How did you gather the strength? How did your routine change? Do you remember telling yourself anything specific about the most badass time of your life?

GETTING COMFORTABLE WITH MONEY

For centuries, even if women worked, men were primarily in charge of the household money. Whether from habit or tradition, that's how it has continued for a long time. While a lot of men are good at being in charge of the money, their gender does not necessarily mean they are better at handling money than women.

I've heard many stories of women who thought their man was managing the household money well. In all actuality, they weren't the good stewards they claimed to be, and sometimes, the husbands were awful at managing money and even worse at investing. Other times, they were doing shitty things like taking money out of the 401(k) to pay for expensive toys or using part of their salary to take their secret girlfriend to Hawaii. While it sounds like I'm man bashing, I'm just acknowledging that things happen in life that aren't always rainbows and butterflies, regardless of who handles the money.

Many times, men are well intentioned, but balancing too many plates in the air to research an investment or figure out which insurance provider to go with. If we're really being honest here, we shouldn't expect anyone to take care of *all* of the finances by themselves. That hardly sounds fair, but it happens more than you would think. Many times, it's not until tragedy strikes that women find out their financial situation is amiss.

When you're not comfortable with your money, and make your man handle all of it, you're telling your money to go away. You're sending a signal to the universe that you really don't care about money and can do without it.

I hate to break this to you, but statistically speaking, women live longer than men. By letting your man handle your money, you are waiting until your circumstances dictate that you *have to be* in charge of your money. This also means that you are forced to figure out your money: where it is, how much you have, and what you want to do with it, all at the same time as a tragedy.

Get comfortable managing your own money *now*, while the pressure is off. Getting familiar with your money means you know where you stand and aren't blindsided when life happens. You know your situation and are comfortable with your numbers. Knowing where you stand financially gives you the knowledge necessary to make solid decisions quickly.

Start to get comfortable with your money. If you're married, get more involved in the conversations your husband is having with the accountant or the financial advisor. Ask him questions about where your money is going, how it's invested, how much you have available in cash.

If you're single, you need to get comfortable with your role as the primary person in charge of your money. Rather than thinking of your money as scary, try to focus on it being exciting. You're in charge of your own destiny, nobody else. You don't need a man to mansplain it to you either. Join a group dedicated to financial empowerment (like my Wealthy Girls Club Facebook group), start to read books about money, put a financial app on your phone, and get informed. All that knowledge will serve you in the long run and, in no time, you'll be more confident about making complex financial decisions.

Chapter 6. Money Mindset—Make Peace with Your Money

When You're Fighting with Your Money, You're Working Against It

Are you fighting with your money? Maybe you're frustrated with your money, or mad that you aren't making headway toward your goals. Rather than continuing to fight with your money, I want you to consider bringing a sense of peace to your money. When you look at your bank account, do you groan or are you happy? Do you feel like you've got it all together?

Many years ago, I found myself groaning out loud every time I looked at my bank account. I groaned at the remaining balance in my account. I felt like I didn't have enough money and the groaning was a result of this huge bummer. I realized that *any* time I checked my bank balance was a big fat bummer. I only saw the number and not the experiences.

What I didn't realize was that every transaction was a wonderful addition to my life: one transaction was date night out with my husband; another was a movie with my son; and another transaction was a delicious dinner with friends. When I added all those experiences together, I realized how blessed I was to have such amazing experiences and people in my life. Thinking about all those wonderful experiences, I couldn't help but be thankful for my financial situation.

Rather than opening up your bank account and groaning or feeling the number that's left in your bank account—after you've paid your bills—isn't big enough, look at the great things that you've done with your money. Even if you just paid bills this month, find gratitude for having enough money to pay those bills. This starts the shift from resenting your money to being grateful for it.

Whenever you have a negative reaction to your money, lean as far into your gratitude as possible. Quickly name three positive things you appreciate about your money and otherwise: maybe you *didn't* get a parking ticket, maybe you found an extra quarter on the street. Even if it's the most minute thing to be grateful for, by leaning into your gratitude you're telling the universe that you want more.

When You Judge Yourself

One of the biggest gifts to give yourself is to stop judging yourself for where you are financially. Where are you is just a point in time; it's not the whole story. A lot of people feel where they are now is where they're going to be for a long time, or even permanently. That's not necessarily the case.

Where are you are now is just a jumping off point. Where you are right now is just a point in time. Every day, you have the opportunity to change your life. If you don't like where you are at this point in time, then put energy into getting to a different place with your money. I've been in a dark place with my money before. It's hard to see past the problems and the bills. Remember you get more of what you focus on, so focus on your possibilities. This will not only get you to start thinking about big goals, but it will also open your mind to what you really want.

I don't think a lot of people take the time to figure out what they *actually* want in life. So, what will it be? What do you really want? Do you want a house in the country? Maybe you want to live in the city in an apartment instead?

You can blame society or even your parents, but it seems like people live their lives by what others want. We think we *should* want a particular thing, like marriage or kids. We often judge ourselves because we want something different, but we're actually living incongruently to what we really want.

This is your life, and you can make it what you want. You owe it to yourself to figure out what you *really* want. Spend some time thinking about it. If you have big lofty long-term, and maybe life-long goals, welcome to the club.

How Do You Make Peace with Your Money When You Have All This Stuff Going On in Your Head?

It's really easy for me just to say, "make peace with your money" and tell you to go on with your day, but this might be hard for some folks. If you're used to fighting your money, beating yourself up for where you are financially, and blocking your abundance, this can be a particularly daunting exercise. Making peace with your money is tough to do because your comfort zone is in the struggle.

I remember sitting in a restaurant on a date with my husband one night. We were talking about money . . . again. My husband was talking about how he was tired of our financial situation. We always seemed to have the same conversation about our money over and over. I said to him, quite matter of factly, "The answer to our question is simple. We just need to be wealthy." He looked at me like I had lost my mind, but then he understood what I was saying. I was done with the struggle and ready for money to be a non-issue.

What I found is that you have to decide you're done with your money struggles. Once this happens, you might quickly find yourself out of your comfort zone. The need to be *done* with the struggle has to be greater than your fear, or bad habits, or insecurities that have kept you in your comfort zone.

In short, you have to decide you're going to make peace with your money, even if that means changing your life. I've always felt there's a special kind of magic in the deciding. So, are you ready to decide to have a different relationship with your money?

THE CONCEPT OF ABUNDANCE

If you've ever heard anyone talk about an *abundance mentality* or the concept of *abundance* or *living in your abundance*, then you know it sounds really woo and abstract. It sounds kind of hippie and vague; however, there is a practicality to it, as well. This is where the woo meets the practical world.

When you live in abundance, you trust that there's more than enough business, money, homes for sale, and everything else to go around. You don't have to stress over all of the details, because there is enough. When I started really leaning into this, I realized that there's an aspect of trust and letting go to living in abundance. I didn't have to be in charge of every little thing, I trusted that there was more than enough for me. In short, I was able to loosen my death grip on the wheel and assume that my life was headed in the right direction.

Some of you are reading this thinking that you have bills to pay, and rent is due next week, and how is that going to happen? Oh, I get it. The thing that is really interesting about believing in abundance is that it's not until you acknowledge you are part of a bigger universe—and that it's OK to rely on the universe to help bring you what you need—that you can let go of some of the worry. In short, life gets a little bit easier.

To learn more about the concept of abundance and abundance mentality, go to: www.victoriasexton.com/createabundance.

How Do You Embrace Your Abundance?

It's important to acknowledge when you're in scarcity mode. If you're panicked that you aren't going to have any clients by the end of the month, and you're not too sure how you're going to pay your rent or there never seems to be enough money in your checking account, that's scarcity. It feels tight, restrictive, and almost desperate.

When you're in scarcity mode, it's near impossible to live in abundance because you're too busy freaking out. Sometimes, just acknowledging that you're freaked out helps take the fear out your money. And other times, you need to dig deeper. If scarcity mentality is the mode that you're used to being in most of the time, and it feels comfortable to you, it may be a little tougher for you to get used to the fact that everyday life can be easier.

The trick is being able to feel if you're in a state of either abundance or scarcity. I try my best to call myself on my bullshit and acknowledge when I'm feeling scarcity. During times where I'm feeling scarce, I grab my journal and try to work out my feelings on paper. We all feel scared or panicked occasionally, but we don't have sit with those feelings forever. During these times, a mantra can be helpful. It helps remind you of the personal goals you're working toward. Some of my favorites are *easy money* or *money easily flows to me*. This reminds me that I have a choice, and I don't have to stress or struggle in making money because money is going to come to me in ways that I hadn't even anticipated.

WHAT'S YOUR MONEY MANTRA?

You can absolutely steal my money mantra *easy money* if it resonates with you, but sometimes, it's more powerful and personal when you develop your own mantra. Include why you've decided to embrace your money, an abundance attitude, and *why* you want to be in this new place financially.

The *why* is really important. Your why reminds you of the reason you're making all these hard changes when your journey gets rough. Life is not easy-peasy all the time. Having a catch phrase to remind you of your big juicy goals, hopes, and dreams can help you through the days when life seems to kick you in the teeth.

A year before my husband I sold our money pit, we were both working for a huge company with great jobs, and we were broke. In one week, between the plumber and the roofer, we spent $45,000. It was a pretty dark time for me. Things felt heavy and there didn't seem to be any end in sight to the home repairs and our financial mess.

In June of 2017, I declared to my husband that it didn't matter what was happening in the world, we were going to sell our house. Every weekend for a year, we were knee-deep in home improvements. When we didn't have the cash for home repairs, we used our Lowe's card, and boy, I was thankful we had it. It was a hard time.

The fact that there was going to be end in sight, was my motivation. My goal was to get OUT of the money pit. Every time something else broke or needed repaired, I reminded myself that there was an end in sight.

Having hope is extremely powerful in our lives. That's what your money mantra should do - give you some hope. What's your money mantra?

GRATITUDE: THE SECRET SAUCE

Gratitude is like a signal to the universe. A weird, cosmic thing happens when we acknowledge what we're grateful for; It's like using the flight attendant button to ask for one more ginger ale. Gratitude is a direct line to the universe saying, *I love this thing, please, please bring me ten more things like it.*

This cosmic signal is why it's important to be aware of what we're focusing on. Are we focusing on all the good stuff in our lives? Are we acknowledging the things that we really love in our lives?

Gratitude enables us to appreciate all the little things that we love in our lives. It's not only the big things that I'm appreciative of, like family or a house or something like that, being grateful for the tiny things is just as important. The tiny things might very well have been overlooked, like how beautiful the sky is today, or the fact that that your coffee tastes so freaking amazing, or how delicious that cookie tastes. It all matters.

For me, gratitude has to be part of my daily routine. Gratitude goes hand in hand with abundance. When I ask for more of the things that I love, they may not always come to me, but it's like that saying *you don't get what you don't ask for*. If there's a higher probability of me getting the things in life I really want, I don't know about you, but I'll take all the short cuts.

Name five things you're thankful for right now. If you really want to get into your gratitude, name five small things and five big things. Maybe you're having a really good hair day. Maybe your meal was amazing. Try to find as many small things as possible that make your life fun as well as special.

YOUR PERMISSION SLIP

For some reason, women have a hard time giving ourselves permission to do the things we *really* want to do. Sometimes what we want isn't conventional or maybe it's not for everyone. That's OK.

I've found that in our culture wanting to have more money is either vilified or revered. This may be just one reason that women have a hard time asking for what they want. I've wanted the kind of life that's comfortable. My older son called me bougie, but I think that I just like nice things. I love good food and traveling and staying in beautiful places. For a long time, I felt almost ashamed of this. I would travel and tell very few people where I would stay or what I would do. Rather than being proud of myself that I could afford such a life, I felt embarrassed. It was such a weird thing to be shameful of.

It wasn't until I gave myself permission to be bougie and fancy and all the things that I wanted to be, that I felt OK with what I wanted, and more than that, who I am.

For some people, they haven't given themselves permission to be who they want, to have the kind of money they want, maybe because their friends will be jealous, or their parents will think that they've changed. It can be hard to finally admit to those closest to you who you truly are share the part of yourself that you've been hiding from the world.

If you haven't already given yourself permission to thrive financially, now is the time. You have the ability to change your financial future. You also have the ability to change the dynamic that you've had with your money in the past. When you decide that you're going to make a change in your life, you give yourself permission.

Whatever your reason for wanting to change your dynamic, relationship, and situation with your money, meaning you want more money, write it down. Use my fill in the blank sentence below to get a handle on what you really want.

I fully give myself permission to _____ because I want a life that is _____.

What role do you want money to play in your life? Maybe you want a different job where you get to travel the world. Or, maybe you want to make more money so that you can hire a cleaning lady, a virtual assistant, or maybe you just want to feel less stressed out when you think of your money.

Many times, we have a hard time giving ourselves permission. We give others permission, but don't always give ourselves the same leeway. If that's you, I'm giving your permission to do anything that you want to do with your life and your money. Maybe you want to pursue a different career, or move to a new location, or do something that your heart has been telling you to do for years. Life is short, give yourself permission.

Believe That It's Possible

For change to happen, you need to believe it's possible. You can say affirmations out the wazoo, but if you don't *feel* it, no matter how many affirmations you say, it's not going to come to fruition.

What do you believe is possible for you? For your life? A lot of people want to believe that amazing things are possible, but secretly they're waiting for the other shoe to drop. That kind of belief system won't serve you at all. If you don't believe that wealth is possible for you, you won't ever achieve it.

I don't know about you, but I want my money to multiply like rabbits. I want my money to provide me the ability to have an awesome life. I challenge you to think about what you really want, too. While you're dreaming up what's possible, get specific. Maybe you want a bigger house or maybe you want a different car or maybe you want to be able to leave your kids an inheritance one day. Our brains are extremely powerful, and when we use them to help create the kind of life that we want, we're actually designing our life.

I can tell you my relationship with my money isn't always easy, but if I don't ask for what I want, and believe that it's possible for me, it won't happen.

Believe that good things are possible and they're coming to you *right now*.

Baby Steps

Do you know those people, who on January 1st, are ready to go with their *new life*? They bought the P90X box set, meal plan, and joined a support group? Are those people still working out in June? Most of them aren't. The reason is that it's hard to change your life, especially overnight.

I'm a big fan of baby steps. It may take you a little while to change the dynamic with your money and how you view it, because of that the most important thing to focus on is not the money per se, but making progress. The baby steps are small wins each day that lead you to your future.

One of the best things you can focus on is good habits. Establishing healthy habits can be difficult, but it gives you a solid financial foundation for your future. Foundational financial habits are going to serve you long after you've stopped struggling with your current money issues. The reason I like to focus on habits is because once you start to see success with your money habits, you can up-level your habits as time goes on.

As you're getting your feet wet with baby steps, make sure you do *not* judge yourself. If you feel like you're not doing things perfectly, or you aren't where you want to be, that's OK. Focus on the process, not just the result.

Give yourself some grace, too. It took me a long time to figure out my money junk, and for my entire adult life my profession has included working with money. You would think that I would have gotten over my own money junk years ago, but it took me a while to figure out a process and a system that works for me. It's going to take you a minute to figure that out too, so make sure you give yourself some grace along the way.

Chapter 7. Energy Is Money, Money Is Energy

The Energy of Making Money

There's an energy around the act of making money that is completely addictive to me. The energy of money making is almost electric and has a certain momentum to it. Making money requires a certain amount of energy. The energy is creative, exciting, and almost happy. If you're trying to make money, and you find that it's such a slog, maybe you need to change how you view the process. When making money, and getting new clients, if it's especially difficult, I find that it's best to step back and loosen the reins a little bit. Maybe you were trying to *make* something happen, but it's not happening the way you planned. Oh boy, I've been there, but I can honestly say that by trying to make it happen, it's going to be a lot harder than just focusing on having fun while you're in the process.

When in the creative flow and excited about making money, the most important thing is keeping your energy flowing. Don't let your momentum slow down. Sometimes, when we're in the energy of making money, we don't get what we want right away. I've heard this referred to as *planting seeds*. You don't plant a seed and then expect a huge tree to grow immediately. The plant needs time to get established. Rather than focusing on getting money now, focus on planting seeds. The energy around planting seeds is still light and fun and energetic and electrifying, but it doesn't have the same amount of expectation that trying to create immediate income does.

Sometimes the energy of being serious with your money, slows things down and can be really frustrating. This is what happens when you try to *make* money happen, *make* sales happen, *make* your business happen, *make* a job happen. When you try to make things happen, you're not in the flow of money. Instead, you're trying to force the flow to do what you want it to do. You can imagine how well that turns out.

There's something about a light, fun energy that helps things to manifest. Try not to take things too seriously. Plant your seeds, have fun, and lean into your joy. You'll be amazed to see what plants grow.

Money Responds to What You're Asking For

Money shows up in the most interesting, different, and weird places when I've asked the universe for additional money. Your money is connected with what you're asking for, or you might say what you're praying for, or what you have your intentions set on.

Sometimes abundance comes in forms that we weren't expecting or from people we weren't expecting, so keep an eye out for money coming from unexpected places. It might be the money you asked for.

While we're on the subject of asking the universe for money, let me touch on the fact that nothing in this world happens on our time. I'll give you an example of this: When I started working with people and their money one-on-one, I noticed right away I had people who wanted to work with me, but they would drag their feet to make an appointment. They would stall for months to years on making the appointment.

The stall tactic really didn't have anything to do with me, and my abilities. It was about them. They didn't feel ready to move forward. The timing was not up to me, it was always up to my client. This was a lesson to me; things don't always happen when we want then or expect them to happen. Sometimes things just don't happen on our time.

Sometimes, we ask and ask and ask and ask for what we want. Maybe it's that new job or the new house that we want. Many times, we hold on to a picture of what the expectation is going to look like when we receive it. When we do that, we're actually blocking our abundance, because we're blocking the possibility of abundance coming to you in ways you hadn't expected. I can remember asking—and asking and asking and asking—the universe for more money in my life in the form of a new job. Then suddenly, I got a huge check in the mail. I was still upset that I didn't get what I was asking for. I received my money; it just wasn't in the form that I wanted or expected.

If we lived in a perfect world, I would tell you to just let go of your expectations and ask for what's best in your life. And while that is the ideal, it's super freaking hard. After I started my business, I immediately wanted new clients. Again, I asked and asked for new clients, but what did I get? I got pre-approved for a business loan, and not just one pre-approval came, but 10, and they kept on coming. I had my abundance and my money; it just didn't come in the form that I wanted.

If you can let go of your expectations, ask for what you want, and be grateful as you patiently await the arrival of it, you're ahead of the game.

You Can Easily Block Your Abundance and Not Even Know It

I can block my abundance in about 2.5 seconds. I honestly didn't even know this was a thing, until I started to recognize it. Now I call myself on it, and lucky for me, I have friends who call me on it, too.

Remember the lady who asked me to put together a custom crystal bag for her? I was shocked that she wanted to pay me for something that (a) isn't my primary profession and (b) I would do even if I didn't get paid for it. Abundance isn't always in the form that you expect. Don't worry about the form that your abundance comes in. Just accept it and be grateful.

Just like you and I have our own energy, money has its own energy. For me, the energy of making money is fun, fast paced, joyful, and playful. Making money has an electrifying energy. You will never magnify your money and your money-making capabilities by being bitter or negative about your money. Resentfulness doesn't breed joy, happiness, or fun, much less money.

One of the weird things that happens for me when I tap into my joy and I get excited about what I'm doing, regardless of the outcome, is *that's* when money comes to me. When I'm super concentrated on making money, I just end up getting frustrated. Try to let go of the expectations and outcomes of your money. Instead, focus more on the joy and playfulness of what you're doing. The whole playfulness aspect of your money is not something that you think about when you think about money. After all, money seems serious and almost masculine, but when you are excited, joyful, and playful, you send a signal to the universe that you want more of what you're doing and what you're getting (aka: money, opportunities, and abundance).

Money is an amplifier and a mirror to what you're focused on and appreciate. The more you are grateful for your money, the more money you will receive in return. The more resentful, frustrated, and angsty you are, the more you'll receive resentment, frustration, and angst in return. Whatever we concentrate on, we will receive more of.

Money Is Easy When You're in the Flow

Working in the flow is so much easier than struggling through your work. Have you ever experienced a time when you're working, doing something you enjoy, or working in your profession and you're just *getting. work. done*? Maybe you have your favorite music playing, but you have a rhythm to your work. You're productive, and you're doing your best work. That's being in the flow.

That same flow is how I want you to feel about your money. When you're in the flow of your money, life is so much easier. You don't worry about money all the time. You're able to let go of your money concerns and accept the abundance that's comping to you.

How do we get into the flow of money? How can we make things easier on ourselves? Just like you set yourself up for success by being in the flow of your work, you also need to set yourself up for success with your money. Get organized, set aside time each week to check your money. Follow through with all those good habits you know about but don't actually make time for. Set up an environment where you can be in the flow.

As the term *flow* might indicate, a sense of letting go is involved with being in the flow of money. It's like that saying *go with the flow*. As a self-proclaimed control freak, I can tell you it's hard to try to control a situation and also be in flow. For things to be light and easy with our money, we need to stop taking ourselves so seriously. A light and easy feeling around our money helps us to get in the flow. When I start to freak out over a situation, I cannot stay in the flow. This is why I try to recognize as quickly as possible when I'm out of flow with my money, so I can get back into the flow.

Find a way to enjoy your money. You can fake this for a bit by leaning into gratitude, but it's also important to separate your money issues from your money itself. Shit happens, and that's not your money's fault. You don't need to blame anyone to start over, and we can start over with our money.

The Energy of Generosity, Stinginess, and Being a Control Freak

Just like there's an energy to making money, there's also an energy to generosity. When we're generous and don't expect anything in return, it feels good, doesn't it?

When you are truly generous with your money, there's a certain high vibe that comes with it. It's like you're giving a little piece of yourself along with your generous gift. There's also an energy in being stingy or miserly. I always think of Ebenezer Scrooge, from *A Christmas Carol*, when I think of the word *miserly*. The energy of stinginess and being miserly feels stiff, and stagnant, like you need to open a window.

Sometimes, when we are super focused on trying to make money, we take ourselves out of the flow of money. We do this by giving all our energy to our frustration and become resentful of our current money situation. We're actually ignoring all the good things going on around us, and we can't see all of the good things happening.

If you have a history of being miserly, find a way to be generous. What's a charity that you love? If donating money seems like it's too much for you right now, donate your time. Try to be more generous with family and friends. You don't need to hand them a wad of cash, instead have friends over for dinner or make another gesture to show them that you care. This switches up the energy of your money.

Sometimes, when we're focused on our own money, and our money situation, we miss out on an opportunity to be generous toward other people. Here's a news flash for you, the saying, *he with the most cash wins*, is just something that someone made up. It's not actually true. We were not put on this earth to make as much money as we possibly can and then die. If you have an opportunity to positively impact somebody else's life, do it.

When we try to hold on to things so tight, it's generally because we're afraid to lose them. We have an illusion of control. Speaking as a control freak, I can tell you that you just have to trust the universe has got you. When you try to control the situation, you end up blocking your abundance. The more you learn to let go of the outcome, the more you can except the money to flow.

Chapter 8. Easy Money Principles

Stop Making Things So Complicated

Isn't it shitty to say, *you need to stop making things so complicated*? It does sound like a low blow, especially when you're struggling with your money. But here's the thing, we as human beings have this pesky habit of making things super complicated, and complicated doesn't help anything. The whole point of *effortless money* is that it's simple!

For a long time, I thought money had to be complicated. It sounds complicated, right? A lot of my clients struggle with the same thing. The articles in the Wall Street Journal and the newscasters on CNBC make financial concepts seem over our heads. Between the financial jargon and economic concepts, it's easy to feel like we just don't get it.

Here's the reality: financial jargon makes money sound complicated and scary. Between the jargon, fear of looking stupid, and not knowing what questions to ask, we can be left feeling like money is too complicated for us to understand. That kind of thinking just keeps us small, as if we're incapable of managing our own money, and that's simply not true.

How do we start to make things less complicated?

1. <u>Put everything in one location and get it organized.</u>

When your financial information is all over the place, it can be difficult to know where you stand. It's also difficult to put your energy toward moving forward and making good financial decisions because you're always wondering where that paper went or what happened to that 1099 you need for your taxes. If you don't have a system for holding your papers or electronic files, it's easy for things to go off the rails.

If you're one of those people that isn't very organized with your financial documents, start with a shoebox. Put all your financial documents in the shoebox.

Do the same thing with electronic files. Save email receipts as a PDF to a file marked *shoebox*. Everything is in one of two locations: the physical shoebox or the file marked shoebox. Once you have all your information in one place, you can sort through what you have. Maybe you don't need to keep all the paperwork.

One of my biggest frustrations with my own money is paper. I hate paperwork and I frequently just throw stuff on my desk or put a file on my computer desktop and don't keep up with my organization. It quickly turns messy, so I try to be super diligent and put my e-files in the right file location and put my paperwork in a central location. This helps me in the long run.

If you want to get really fancy, go to www.victoriasexton.com and you'll find my financial organizer worksheets there. These can help you get a little bit more organized and have everything in one location. You can also do this on your own by creating your own system. It's totally up to you. Regardless, get ready to streamline your financial paperwork, bills, electronic information, and any other financial information you need.

I helped my mother clean out her parents' house, and when she passed, I cleaned out her house. I can tell you that you don't need that phone bill from 1985. You probably don't need the phone bill from last month. Everything is online. I can pretty much guarantee whomever you have a bill with has a record of it. If you really need a copy of the bill, you can always scan it and keep it on your computer.

I also recommend sifting through your electronic files at tax time. I recently found a car bill from five years ago on my hard drive, and I don't even have that car anymore. Paper and electronic files are just one more thing to sift through. It's a distraction to reaching your financial goals and is a time suck.

Set parameters for yourself. Do you want to keep annual statements only? Or a copy of the bill until you know it processed? Determine if you want to keep everything or nothing at all. Remember, the system is supposed to be easy. What is easiest for you? If you don't know the answer to that question, just try something and see if that works. If it doesn't, you can try something else in a month or two.

2. Ignoring your bills won't make them any smaller.

I know a lot of people, even myself at times, are prone to ignore their financial situation. If you ignore the situation, it seems less scary, because you don't feel the gravity of the whole situation, or maybe you think the situation will resolve itself. I can guarantee it never works out that way.

Ignoring your money is in *no way*, going to help you. If you're one of those people who gets your credit card bill, doesn't open it, and stashes it in your desk drawer because you're afraid, at some point in time you need face it. Many times, the reason we're afraid to look at the bill doesn't even have to do with the actual bill, it has to do with what it represents or how it makes us feel.

When my husband and I were going through a hard time financially, due to our house falling apart, I avoided looking at my credit card, because the balance never seemed to go down. I felt trapped in a financial situation I didn't know how to get out of and looking at the bill only solidified that feeling.

If you're avoiding your money, just know this: the balance will never get smaller, the interest rate will never go down, and the loan will never get paid off earlier if you never look at your statement. As painful as it can be to look at the paperwork right now, the long-term ramifications of ignoring your money are much more painful. Not only is there a practical ramification of ignoring your finances but there's an energetic one as well. When you ignore your money, you're telling the universe it's not important to you, hence you don't want it. The result of this maybe you sending signals to the universe that are incongruent with what you really want, which (for everyone) is more money.

For the sake of your future, you have to stop ignoring your money and get an understanding of your financial situation. I can guarantee you have more life to live than you ever anticipated, and no one ever woke up and said, *oh damn, I have too much money*. This is why we have to do the hard work of making sure we're taken care of in the future. I refer to this as taking care of my future self, but we'll talk about that in a minute. For me to be happy and wealthy in the future, it's worth some current discomfort of looking at my bills now.

You owe it to yourself to do this hard work of paying attention to your money. You can do this by making things lighter and easier. Turn on your favorite music while you pay the bills. Set a kitchen timer for ten minutes and dive in. Dedicate those few minutes to looking at your numbers. When you're done, make sure you give yourself a big treat and a pat on the back.

3. Make it easy for people to give you money.

One of the best things you can do for yourself is to make it easy for people to give you money. For example, if your employer wants to pay you through a check, can they do direct deposit? If you're a business owner, reevaluate how easy it is for someone to pay you. Remember our mantra is *effortless money*. We want everything about your money to be as easy as possible, and that includes how you will receive your money.

Set up PayPal and Venmo accounts. Again, it's one of the easiest and quickest ways to can accept payment.

4. Take action, even if you don't want to.

Taking action can be the hard part. Sometimes we just don't want to spend time on our finances. If you give me the option of going to lunch with my friends or financial planning, I'll pick lunch every time ... and I love helping people with their money! This is why it's important to build good habits. If you plan to review your finances every Monday at 7:30 a.m., you're much more likely to do it.

I bet we all can list about ten things we need to do in relation to our money that we just haven't done. Like cancel that old checking account or call and get a better interest rate on your credit cards. Most of the time these are small and not on the top of our to-do list, but, by not doing these things, we're ignoring our money again.

It's probably going to be uncomfortable the first time you take action. It's going to be uncomfortable the first time you decide to commit to your money and do the not-so-fun things, but it's also going to change how you view your money and how much money is actually in your bank account. Just do it. You'll be happier in the long run that you did.

5. You can't see the label when you're in the jar.

I recently heard this saying and I just had to say, *yes* out loud. Sometimes we can't see the situation for what it is. That's because we're in it. This is the same reason you probably can't see your greatness or see when we're making horrible decisions, though we can see situation for what it is when our friends are making bad choices.

This is the reason why therapists have therapists and life coaches have life coaches. Sometimes we all need some support and discernment. If this is you, know that there's support available. I, or someone who does financial coaching like I do, can be a great resource.

Align Your Money with Your Mindset

One of the biggest areas I see people take a misstep is in their money mindset. There's a misconception that if someone has a positive money mindset, they don't get scared, feel uncertain, or nervous about their money, and they certainly don't make any money mistakes. They just meditate and are super calm, knowing all is well. There's no part of that picture that's realistic.

I've found that my money mindset requires a refresh on a consistent basis. Some days I feel like I've done everything wrong. Some days I feel like things aren't working out as anticipated. I have to remind myself that in today's perfect Instagram-selfie society, authenticity is scarce, making it easy for you to feel like you're the only one not doing things right. It's totally normal to feel like you don't have life figured out.

Here's something to remember: part of your mindset is embracing your abundance, being hopeful about the future, and believing that good things are not only possible, but they're coming to you. Some days I live my abundance All. Day. Long. Other days, it's hard for me to stop beating myself up over forgetting to pay the PG&E bill.

The process of doing inner work is never easy. Inner work requires introspection, the ability to change our behaviors, and a desire to do better. Be confident that you are learning skills and furthering yourself financially. All those things are progress.

Rather than beating yourself up, recognize where you are. Come up with a money mantra for when you're feeling like it's all falling apart. Anchor to the knowing that progress is sometimes slow, but 365 days of progress adds up to big changes in the end.

Chapter 9. Your Inner Wealthy Woman

What Does "Wealthy" Mean to You?

Everyone has a different definition of what "wealthy" means. To some people, it means you're living like Beyoncé and shopping on Rodeo Drive every week. For other people, being wealthy means you're not stressed about money every day and you're able to pay your bills without wondering where the money is going to come from. The trick here is to figure out what wealthy means to you.

I recommend establishing your own definition for the word "wealthy," because if we don't know what "wealthy" is, how can we ever attain it? For most people, "wealthy" is this far off goal that can't be attained by regular folks, but really, "wealthy" can mean whatever you want it to mean. The trick here is knowing what you want.

This exercise gets complicated for folks because they don't know what they actually want. We're told by society (ahem, advertising) that we *should* want a fancy fast car, or a huge house, or we *should* want to be super famous. It's those types of messages that lead us to believe we would be happier if we just achieved external success, and that's not necessarily true.

The big questions to ask yourself while you're thinking about *wealthy* are: What do you really want from life? Do you want to live in the Florida Keys and sit in the sun all day? Do you want to live in a big city and have a retirement business? Do you want to own your own business? Do you want to chase the career you've always dreamed of ? Do you want to quit the job you have now?

When we spend some time quietly checking in with ourselves about what we want, we end up figuring out what *we* want versus what everybody else thinks we should want. Nobody else is living your life but you, so make sure you are striving for what you want.

For a long time, I have wanted to own my own business. I was one of those employees who would say, "That initiative doesn't seem like a good idea." or "Why are we doing this project?" and I would have to find it within me to be a good little soldier and do what my boss asked me to do. For years, I had this dream to quit my day job and do something on my own, but having your own business is not for the faint of heart. I knew it would be hard, and I also knew some people in my life would have heartburn over me quitting a perfectly good job just because it didn't make me happy. For a long time, I kept this secret dream to myself. I kept working for other people because of the good health insurance and other benefits, but deep down inside, I was slowly dying.

I had to really ask myself, *what do I want*? What I realized was that no part of me wanted to work for someone else, especially someone who didn't get my vision. That soul-searching was essential to my growth as a human being and as an entrepreneur. I never would have gathered up the guts to start my own business if I didn't come to the realization that I couldn't continue to work for somebody else and be happy.

I'll ask you again, what do you really want? This is such an important question. I can't stress enough to you the importance of knowing what you want, and what's going make you happy. Even if you don't know the end goal, knowing the next step lands you closer to what you do want then where you were before.

Envision Your Inner Wealthy Woman

Now that you figured out what you want, what is the wealthy you going to do? For a long time, people like athletes have used visualization to help them picture how they are going to cross the finish line. They use visualization to prepare to win that race. I like to use visualization for my own goals, as well. It's free, quick, and can be very powerful.

I went to a life coaching seminar with a friend of mine, much to my chagrin. I honestly did not feel like the seminar was my jam and I didn't want to be there. I realized we were stuck there, because so few people were in attendance. It was one of those situations where it would be awkward to get up and leave, so we stayed and had a big group coaching session. It all felt like too much for me. I had my own crap going on and didn't really have time for this huge group coaching thing. We got to the midway point of the seminar and I was still convinced that I was not supposed to be there. Clearly, this is for everybody else, and not for me, right?

After coming back from our break, the instructor had us do a guided meditation. She had us close our eyes and imagine what we would be like in five years if we had achieved all our financial goals. The instructor continued to lead us through the mediation; she had us imagine ourselves in the future. She told us to ask our future selves some questions. As much as I didn't want to do the exercise, I found I was not only able to connect with the wealthy future me, but that version who was an entrepreneur and successful and seemed like she had it all together. I saw the version of me who was wealthy and didn't have a care in the world concerning her finances.

Here's the thing that was so interesting to me about this exercise: First of all, I was impeccably dressed, with amazing hair, and looked ageless. It's my fantasy, right? So, I looked amazing, like I had money and a stylist to help make sure I wasn't going to wear something awkward (which is something I would normally do). The second thing that was interesting was the instructor told us to ask our future selves questions and get life advice from her.

The irony was amazing. This was the exercise that I really did *not* want to do, but I learned so much from having a conversation with my future self. I found that I was not only able to connect with the future version of me, but I was also able to connect with the *wealthy successful* version of me. I was able to connect with the version of myself who is successful and wealthy and didn't have a care in the world about her finances. I had connected with my inner wealthy woman.

Then, halfway through the meditation, I fell asleep. I ended up doing one of those head bob things and woke myself up. Thankfully, no one else noticed.

Driving home from the event, I felt like a jackass for having made fun of the exercise. Clearly, I had something to learn. I realized this exercise was about more than just meditation, this exercise was about visioning who you've always wanted to be.

Visualization can be a game changer to successfully achieving your financial goals. Just like athletes have been visualizing running across the finish line, business professionals use this same technique to visualize giving a great presentation or closing a new business deal. Visualization is extremely powerful, and you can use it to help you achieve your goals.

This step is fundamental, but often lost on people when planning financial goals. Many times, people have lofty goals, but if they can't picture themselves reaching those goals, how do they ever expect to achieve them?

The exercise of concentrating on your future self, really struck a chord with me. I find that when I'm having a hard time figuring out the next step, talking with friends or family isn't always helpful, especially when their own issues and insecurities begin to surface. If you're able to tap into your future self, the person who loves you unconditionally and wants what's best for you, you'll always get advice that's ideal for you.

The next time you're having a dilemma, tap into your future self, sit in a quiet place for a while and see what your future self has to say about the situation.

To find out more about meditation and to grab a copy of my wealthy woman guided meditation go here: www.victoriasexton.com/meditation/.

Chapter 10. Your Wealth & Your Woo

People always get confused when I talk about woo. If you were to look up the definition of "woo," you would see something like: "unconventional spiritual beliefs, maybe spirituality, or belief in a higher power."

Money woo is my own particular label for the things you believe in relation to your money. Our brains are super powerful, and belief can change everything. If you don't believe you will ever get out of your financial situation; if you believe that your crappy financial scenario will last forever, then it will. If you believe you're going to make an impact and have a different life, eventually, it will happen. Regardless of what you believe, the connection between belief and your financial situation is very strong.

When I talk about *money woo*, it's more than just believing; It's also about tapping into your abundance, knowing what you want out of life, and asking the universe for it. I mean, how can we ask for what we want, if we don't know what it looks like?

This is a concept that some people really do not believe in. Many people think you go out, get a job, and that's it. To them, there's no spiritual connection at all. Well friends, that doesn't explain a whole crap ton of things that happen on the regular. For example, why is it that the people who just know they are going to *change their lives* actually do it, and the people who believe nothing good is possible for them? They end up getting that, too.

Place Your Cosmic Order

I have a friend who always says, "Have you placed your cosmic order?" Meaning, do you know what you specifically want and are you asking for it? This is really the first step to manifesting anything. I remember when I manifested my current car. I wanted a Chevy Tahoe, but it really wasn't in my budget. I was looking at smaller cars and I just didn't find what I wanted. My oldest son finally said, "Mom, why don't you just get what you want?"

I thought to myself *Yea, why don't I just get what I want*?

So, I decided to manifest what I wanted, and that was a Tahoe. I wrote down all the specifications of the car, down to the add-ons. I was focused on the fact that it was coming to me. My Tahoe was going to actualize in my life.

In July I went to a car dealership. I talked to the salesman and told him what I wanted. He thought it was a pretty tall order. He even said, "I'm sorry ma'am, but we don't normally get cars like that in with those kinds of details." He very nicely told me that he would call me if he got a car like that in the dealership.

Much to his surprise, he called me in October to tell me a car with my exact specifications, just arrived on the lot. There was the car, my Tahoe, with the mileage I wanted, within the years I specified, and within my price range. I just knew it was meant to be. I asked him for financing and the interest rate was amazing. The whole process at the dealership only took an hour, and if you've ever purchased a car, you know it's an all-day thing. Don't even ask me why it takes all freaking day to buy a car—it always does—but not my Tahoe. It was such an awesome example of something I wanted and manifested in my life.

I'm using this example so you understand there's a connection between woo, belief, and money. Sometimes that connection is hard to explain to people. When I tell the story of my Tahoe, people are shocked and surprised because it was so specific.

I'm not telling you that story to brag, I'm telling you the story to let you know that it's possible to ask to be in a different financial situation, believe it will happen, and have it come to fruition. It is possible, but you need to believe it.

Listen to Your Gut... Especially About Your Money

I can't tell you how many times I've heard from women "I knew my marriage wasn't going to work out before the wedding." or "I had a feeling that my business partner was a shady guy." or "I just knew that job wasn't going to work out." I could go on and on with examples.

Our gut is talking to us all the time, and we rarely listen. What's more, people don't seem to think their gut is talking to them about their money. It's as if they only have a gut reaction about certain things, and money isn't one of them.

Listening to your gut concerning your money is especially helpful. Sometimes things seem good on paper, but they may not be good for you, personally. You never know, maybe something better is on its way to you.

How do you listen to your gut about your money? Your gut talks in a whisper. If you want to hear it loudly, it's best to get quiet: meditate, journal, walk, hike, be in nature. You can distract yourself with Netflix all day long, but you won't be able to listen to your gut that way. Make time each day to listen to your gut. That way, it will become one of your good money habits.

Chapter 11. How to Keep It up, Even When It All Falls Apart

Upgrade, Please

What I'm about to say is probably the worst thing for someone to hear when everything is falling apart: sometimes it needs a full *apart* to build something really amazing. We have to realize, sometimes the door is closed shut, and we can't go through it anymore, so we have to find another door. That type of scenario can be painful, especially when there's no other door to go through, and it feels like you have to squeeze through a window.

I quit my safe, soul-sucking corporate job to become a financial advisor. Becoming an advisor required me to get several licenses prior to employment. It was a bit of undertaking, but I was happy to do the work and prepare for my next career.

I was at a corporate training, the month after I received my licenses. I was there with 50 other new advisors in navy blue suits. It was then that I realized the job was not right for me. I had worked so hard to get all my securities licenses to make sure my i's were dotted and t's were crossed. I started talking with our corporate offices about some of my ideas, but the company rejected them all. I had to strictly play by their rules. I had to follow their guideline and that's it. There was no room for me to be creative.

I was incredibly disappointed and tried for a while to play by the corporate rules. I tried to fit into their box of what was expected of me. The problem is when you're a unicorn among horses, it's easy for the horses to see you're not into following the rest of the pack.

What I didn't realize was, for me, that job needed to come entirely apart before I would quit. I needed to realize that the job wasn't right for me before I would be willing to go out on a limb and open my own business. Essentially, my old dream had to die before my new dream could come to fruition.

Sometimes we feel stuck, and our energy feels stagnant. Everything about us feels like we can't move on. That feeling of being stuck is one of the most awful feelings you can have, but on the other side of being stuck is an upgrade. We can't have a major life upgrade without our old life completely blowing up.

When your life falls apart, it's an opportunity to rebuild, and decide which parts of your current life you really want to keep and which ones to upgrade. When your life seems like it's crumbling, my advice is to let it all fall apart. You're due for an upgrade.

The Antidote to Being Stuck Is Action

If you're feeling stuck, the antidote is to take action. Part of the problem with being stuck is, you don't know which action to take. Everything seems like the wrong move. The thing with getting unstuck is you need to make a choice and run with it. You just need to try something, and if you don't like it, then try something else.

Even though being stuck is one of the most horrible feelings in the world, it can also be a blessing to realize what you're doing isn't working anymore. That job you've had for years is no longer serving you. The relationship you've been unhappy in, maybe it's not giving you what you need.

The key to getting unstuck is to recognize exactly where you're stuck, and then take action. It also helps if you try to keep things lighthearted. I know firsthand how being stuck really sucks. The whole thing makes you want to lay on the couch and watch Netflix all day, but you can't do that. We have work to do. You need to realize that being stuck is just a state of being and that state will pass.

Focus on Progress, Not Perfection

It's also easy to get down on ourselves for not being perfect savers or being overachievers. It's easy to focus on the numbers. The reality is we are only in control of are our mindset and our actions. When you get right down to it, the only things we can control are the actions we take and how we feel about them. The rest of what happens in our world is not within our control. I personally couldn't control the fact that in 2020 we had a pandemic. I couldn't control the fact that the schools closed down, and overnight, I became a school teacher, short-order cook, and mom trying to work from home. What I could control was my attitude, the actions I was taking, the connections I was making with people, and what plans I was putting in motion. And that's pretty much it.

When you look at your numbers, sometimes it's a huge bummer. If you're not a patient person, and I understand because I have very little patience, it's easy to judge yourself. Don't. Progress feels slow and frustrating, but that's part of the process. It's like turning a huge ship, it takes a while to turn the whole ship around. Rather than judge yourself for where you are, focus on your habits. Focus on the things that you can control and reward yourself for creating really good habits. These habits are the first step to creating wealth. Most of the time people who are wealthy did not become wealthy overnight. They established good habits and spent a lot of time making sure they took steps toward their goals.

Regardless of your bank balance or your credit card balance or how much you owe on your mortgage, focus on establishing habits and reward yourself for sticking with them. It's the habits that will allow you to build wealth in the long run.

Setbacks Happen

Setbacks will happen, regardless of who's at fault. Many times setbacks are the result of circumstance, not the rest of someone acting poorly. Either way, things happen that might cause you to have to regroup or even start over. This is one of the reasons that it's essential to have a plan in place prior to something happening. That way, if you're in the middle of a panic, you've already thought of what to do next.

I call this part of your plan the Setback Plan. It's the part of your financial plan that details what to do if everything falls apart? Yes, this includes your emergency savings, but it also includes your plan of how you'll emotionally support yourself during a hard time.

Part of your setback plan might be to create an inspirational music playlist or to put on your favorite movie where the underdog wins. Come up with a plan for how you'll pick yourself back up when things fall apart.

YOU ARE YOUR NEW BFF

I'd like to introduce you to new your new best friend, and that's you. The most important relationship you have is with yourself. If you beat yourself up all day, you will experience the effects of that. Just like if you give yourself some love and some grace all day, you will experience the effects of that too. When you're venturing out into the world, kicking ass and taking names, give yourself some love. You're doing a great job and you are the only person who knows how hard you've been working.

Cultivating a relationship with yourself is super beneficial. You are the one person who will be with you forever. This is an unfortunate reality of being human.

One relationship I'm always working on, and will continue to work on, is the one that I have with myself. When you're OK with who you are and the things you've achieved, life becomes a lot sweeter. Rather than chasing the *shoulds*—the things other people think you *should* be doing with your life—you're living for you.

We say such awful things to ourselves. We say things we would never say out loud to another human being, yet we say them to ourselves. All that negative self-talk is just junk rolling around in our heads and that head-trash needs to be cleared out.

How do you start cultivating a relationship with yourself if you have never done it before? You have to connect with the deepest part of you; the part that talks to you every day, but you haven't been paying attention to. Spend time with yourself, away from all the chatter. We can distract ourselves with Netflix all day, but we may be missing the signs our body and soul may be sending us. I'm a big believer in signs, but when I'm overly distracted, I can't hear my intuition, much less the signs that the universe is sending me.

We live in a society of distraction, where people would rather be distracted then do the inner work that's required to become the person you were truly meant to be. Start to spend time alone every day. Journaling, yoga, walking, and meditation are all great activities to help you connect with yourself. You, my friend, are a special and unique person. You should be proud of the person you are and the decisions you've made in your life. If you aren't, it's a good time to find out why.

When you know what really makes you happy, what you really want, you gain the courage to follow after it. You need to spend time figuring out what it is you want and why. When you know the answer to that, it's easier to ignore everything else and appreciate yourself for the person you are.

We all have special gifts. If you're aware of what your gift is, ask yourself this question: *Am I using my gifts*? If not, why not? I think about this every time people tell me they chose a job that makes a lot of money over doing something they love. Security over the thing that they're passionate about. I get why people do this. I mean, we all need to pay the rent.

But if you're an artist and you decide to take an office job, how is that office job in alignment with you as an artist? Maybe it is and maybe it isn't. Maybe you're literally just taking the office job to pay the bills and you're going to do your art at night. That's OK, just make sure you're making the best choice for you, and nobody else.

Tools in the Toolbox

What tools are in your toolbox? I'm not talking about the toolbox in the garage, I'm talking about the tools that you have cultivated to make your life easier. One thing I've learned about myself is that I am a little weird, and that weirdness means that my brain works a certain way. For example, I have a running list in my head of things I need to get done; I also have a second list of creative ideas that are in various phases of creation. This is why I have a 5 ft white board in my kitchen. When I'm working out an issue or project, I need the space to lay it out. This is just one of techniques that I have in my toolbox to help me with everyday life.

We're all different—our brains work differently—so it makes sense that we would need different tools in our proverbial toolbox. These tools are going to be different for each person. This is one of the reasons why those Facebook ads we get, about how someone used a system and made $1 million in their business, can be so deceiving. They used a system that worked for them, but it may not necessarily work for you. That may not be the tool that you need in your toolbox.

You have a toolbox that is different and unique compared to anyone else in this world. Your toolbox needs to be filled with the tools *you* can use to be successful in life and with your money. The reason I'm bringing this up is a lot of people feel like they should just buy a system, and if that system doesn't work for them, there's something wrong with them.

There's nothing wrong with you. Sometimes you need a different system. Most people would laugh at my financial system because it's really just a spreadsheet. It's super simplistic, but it works for me. It works for me *because* it is so simple. I don't like complicated systems around money, that's just me. You may need a different system around your money.

As you're working on your financial education and gathering resources, think about what tools you need in your toolbox. Where do you need help specifically? Do you need help preparing your taxes? Do you need help figuring out your monthly bills? Do you need help figuring out a savings plan? Once you know the areas where you need help, you can research and get resources (from people like me) like tools that make sense for you.

Make sure you go to www.victoriasexton.com/resources to grab my list of free tools. Some of them may be great additions to your own toolbox.

Chapter 12. My Wish for You

Get Curious

Have you ever noticed that kids don't get super stressed out? Well, at least most kids. Instead, they get really curious. When my son was a toddler, he was so curious that I used to call him George (like Curious George from the book series). He asked me questions all day long. A lot of times I would tell him, "I don't know why." As a mom, it made me want to buy noise canceling headphones and just nod.

While being asked a million questions can get on your nerves, I also appreciate my son's sense of curiosity. When we have a sense of curiosity, we let our imagination go wild.

It starts with a question like, *How does that work*? Or *I wonder if I can do that*?

By tapping into our sense of curiosity, what we're actually doing is letting our brains run wild for a little bit. Get curious about your money. Get curious about investments. Get curious about how you can make things easier for yourself.

You can even ask yourself this question: *How do I make this easy*?

When my brain wants to run wild and I start to think things in my life are really complicated, I like to ask myself that question.

How can I make things easy?

Most of the time the answer comes to me and I realize there's a way I can make things simpler. Try it and see if that works for you.

TELL YOUR FEAR TO KICK ROCKS

For a long time, fear ruled me. I mean, what if things didn't work out? What if that job ended up being a total nightmare, or the business I wanted to start totally failed? What if? What if? What if? The interesting thing about life is that it's not a linear journey. Somehow, we think it is supposed to be that way: you finish school and then you get a job, and then you get a girlfriend, and then you get married, and then you have kids, etc., but life is not that way.

During the pandemic, at the height of the lockdown, we were all homeschooling. One day my son started reading me a story that he was reading for school. The story was about a cook in the mid-1800s named George Crum.

As the story was told, apparently some jerk at George's restaurant kept sending back his french fries, saying they weren't crispy enough. George clearly had a sense of humor. He sliced the potatoes super duper duper thin, and then fried the heck out of them. As the story goes, the potato chip was born.

My son looked up from the book he was reading and said Best. Mistake. Ever.

Sometimes, good things come out of mistakes or situations that aren't ideal. Sometimes, you have to go through a weird, awkward, uncomfortable, or not-so-great situation to come out on the other side, where you might just realize it was the best mistake ever.

You have to tell your fear to kick rocks if you ever want to get to the other side. You have to find a way to push through the fear and do it, anyway. I'm sure that anyone who's ever started a big adventure has been scared shitless. The key is knowing that regardless of success or failure, it's all a part of the journey, and the journey is really the point.

THE COURAGE TO INVEST IN YOU

Maybe you grew up *never* talking about money. Maybe you came from an environment where everything seemed fine on the outside, but just like the iceberg, there was a lot going underneath the surface. Maybe your mom was worried about saving every last penny, while she acted like she had money to burn when the neighbors were around. Whatever your story is, you can change it.

The secret to changing your story is to start investing in yourself. Investing in yourself looks like taking the course that will qualify you for a new job. Investing in yourself means believing you are smart enough to manage your own money. Investing in yourself means reading books about how you can stay in your power.

Give yourself permission to invest in *you*. You are your most important commodity. There will only be one you, so make sure you're allowing the necessary investment to become the best version of yourself.

The Courage to Do All the Adulting

Some days, adulting is hard. The other day, I was thinking, *what if Peter Pan grew up, and all of a sudden, he's doing his own taxes*? I bet he would think, *this is bullshit, where are the lost boys*?

I'm sorry that adult life involves things like paying your taxes or balancing your checkbook, but that doesn't mean none of these things can be any fun. Find a way to make it lighter and less stressful.

Taking care of your money is actually the most simple form of self-care. You're taking care of your present self and your future self. Your BFF, your wealthy future self is counting on you to do hard things, so you better get to it.

I've talked with many clients in their 20s and they have this misconception that doing *adult type things* is totally boring. You know what's fun: being able to buy an apartment building that's going to give you passive income all friggin' year. That's fun. Having enough residual income to buy a beach house. That's fun.

Along the line somewhere, we, as a society, decided it wasn't fun to be an adult. And yes, there's some not-so-fun things that come with being an adult, but the benefits of adulting are far better than the cost of putting your head in the sand and expecting someone else to take care of it.

Do yourself a favor, start telling yourself that adulting is far more desirable than people have led you to believe. I've always thought that when you're able to take care of yourself, and you don't have to rely upon anybody else, your options open up greatly. Let's get you some options.

Get a Tribe to Support You

Have you ever noticed it's really hard to find time to read books, except if you're a member of a book club. There's something about the peer pressure that helps you to get something done. This is one of the reasons why having a tribe is so effective. I suggest you find like-minded people amongst your group of family and friends, who have the same financial goals as you, or are at least on the same path to improve their financial situation.

When I was in my 20s, I had this friend Jen, and I realized I could no longer afford to hang out with her. Jen and I liked to go to a specific shopping area. We would have Mexican food (and margaritas) and then we would walk over to the mall after two margaritas. Let me just say, this is never a good idea. Drinking and then shopping is a great way to blow your budget. As much fun as it was to hang out with Jen, I realized when I hung out with her, I didn't make solid financial decisions. Instead, I made decisions based upon the fun in the moment.

Nowhere in my budget did I include a spot for margaritas and shopping, but I was spending money like I did. When you have a tribe around you that has similar financial goals, it can become a lot easier to make good financial decisions. If everybody else is working on their finances, suggesting a hike and a picnic over a fancy lunch out goes over better. This is one of the reasons why a tribe is so important; your tribe is there to support you on your journey.

If you don't have a tribe, there are many resources online where you can find people who have the same values and goals as you. Start talking with family, friends, and coworkers to see if any of them have the same goals as you. One of the interesting things about our society is we rarely talk about money, but you can take the awkwardness out of the situation by bringing up the financial goals you're working on. Maybe they have some too. Maybe you guys want to meet up for a money book club?

It's important in any journey to have people who support you along the way. The same goes for your financial journey.

YOUR EFFORTLESS MONEY

My wish for you is that you find your version of effortless money. It's taken me a while to figure out my version of effortless money, too. We're all different. We all have different strengths. We all have different ways of learning and doing things. Don't be afraid to tweak systems or concepts to best suit you. It's your money, manage it any way you like.

You are a spectacular human being. You should be proud of yourself for even being interested in improving your financial situation. Keep reading books about money, articles about money, taking courses about money, and investing in you. You're worth it.

For those of you that need support, go to www.victoriasexton.com/strategy. My specialty is helping those who need support and guidance with their finances. Some of the things my clients say after a strategy session include: "I feel so much better even after one conversation." and "I finally feel confident about my money." and "You make complex financial topics so simple."

About the Author

Victoria Sexton helps women to make their money effortless so they can stop stressing and start making headway toward their financial goals.

Victoria is the founder of Align Wealth Coaching, creator of the Effortless Money System and host of the Don't Play With Trash podcast. After spending years of working in finance and still not meeting her own financial goals, she discovered her own secret sauce, combing money mindset with a straight-forward personal finance system. Now she teaches her clients the same system that allowed her to experience financial freedom.

Victoria helps successful women who are brilliant business women, but aren't too sure what to do with their money, or just don't know where to start. With Victoria's help, clients have gone from confusion and uncertainty to clarity and having a plan. Find out more about how you can work with Victoria by going to www.victoriasexton.com.

Made in the USA
Monee, IL
04 November 2026

67381843R00069